THE AREAS OF MY EXPERTISE

AN ALMANAC OF COMPLETE WORLD KNOWLEDGE
COMPILED WITH INSTRUCTIVE ANNOTATION
AND ARRANGED IN USEFUL ORDER BY ME,

JOHN HODGMAN

A PROFESSIONAL WRITER, IN

THE AREAS OF MY EXPERTISE

WHICH INCLUDE

MATTERS HISTORICAL — MATTERS LITERARY
MATTERS CRYPTOZOOLOGICAL — HOBO MATTERS
FOOD, DRINK, & CHEESE (A KIND OF FOOD)
SQUIRRELS & LOBSTERS & EELS
HAIRCUTS — UTOPIA
WHAT WILL HAPPEN IN THE FUTURE
AND MOST OTHER SUBJECTS

Illustrated with a Reasonable Number of Tables and Figures

AND FEATURING THE BEST OF

"WERE YOU AWARE OF IT?"

JOHN HODGMAN'S LONG-RUNNING
NEWSPAPER NOVELTY COLUMN OF STRANGE FACTS
AND ODDITIES OF THE BIZARRE

"THE ALMANAC THAT CONTAINS NO WEATHER INFORMATION
AND, ONCE PLACED ON YOUR SHELF, WILL SECRETLY REPLACE
ALL NEIGHBORING BOOKS WITH ITS OWN TEXT"

E.P. DUTTON
LOWER MANHATTAN — NEW YORK CITY
2005

DUTTON

Published by Penguin Group (USA) Inc.
375 Hudson Street, New York, New York 10014, U.S.A.

Penguin Group (Canada), 90 Eglington Avenue East, Suite 700, Toronto, Ontario, Canada M4P 2Y3 (a division of Pearson Penguin Canada Inc.); Penguin Books Ltd, 80 Strand, London WC2R ORL, England; Penguin Ireland, 25 St Stephen's Green, Dublin 2, Ireland (a division of Penguin Books Ltd); Penguin Group (Australia), 250 Camberwell Road, Camberwell, Victoria 3124, Australia (a division of Pearson Australia Group Pty Ltd); Penguin Books India Pvt Ltd, 11 Community Centre, Panchsheel Park, New Delhi - 110 017, India; Penguin Group (NZ), cnr Airborne and Rosedale Roads, Albany, Auckland 1310, New Zealand (a division of Pearson New Zealand Ltd); Penguin Books (South Africa) (Pty) Ltd, 24 Sturdee Avenue, Rosebank, Johannesburg 2196, South Africa. Penguin Books Ltd, Registered Offices: 80 Strand, London WC2R ORL, England. Published by Dutton, a member of Penguin Group (USA) Inc.

First printing, September 2005

10 — 9 — 8 — 7 — 6 — 5 — 4

LIBRARY OF CONGRESS CATALOGING-IN-PUBLICATION DATA
HAS BEEN APPLIED FOR.
ISBN 0-525-94908-9
PRINTED IN THE UNITED STATES OF AMERICA
SET IN THE USUAL MANNER
DESIGNED BY SAM POTTS.

THIS REASONABLY PRICED
HARDCOVER DUTTON BOOK
CONTAINS THE COMPLETE TEXT
OF

THE AREAS OF MY EXPERTISE.

*NOT A SINGLE WORD
HAS BEEN OMITTED.*

If you purchased this book without a cover, you should be aware that it was reported as "UNSOLD AND DESTROYED" to the Publisher and is stolen property. Also, you should be aware that the cover was awesome. It featured a painting of a metallic silver dragon flying up either to rescue or eat a beautiful, nearly nude sword maiden as she falls off a cliff. All of this is overseen by the bitter glare of the ever-uncaring Triple Suns. Plus, a very flattering portrait of the Author appeared within the Main Sun.

If you purchased this book with a cover, you should know that this book was accidentally reported as "SOLD AND NOT DESTROYED" to the Publisher, and both the author and the publisher have received payment for it. It is unclear how this may have happened.

But in either case:

Under arrangement with the Publisher, purchasing this book frees you from the obligation to read it.

OFFERED

THIS DAY

with gratitude

TO

KSF

The Metaphysicians of Tlön are not looking for truth, nor even for an approximation of it; they are after a kind of amazement.

Poor Richard's Almanack, 1733 edition

It would take up too much space to enumerate in these prefatory remarks the valuable fund of knowledge to be found here. Suffice it to say, if you are seeking for information of the past, or of any of the facts of today, glance at the table of contents, or "Look within, you will find it."

The World of Wisdom, 1887

The plain Truth of the Matter is, I am excessive poor, and my Wife, good Woman, is, I tell her, excessive proud; she cannot bear, she says, to sit spinning in her Shift of Tow, while I do nothing but gaze at the Stars; and has threatened more than once to burn all my Books and Rattling-Traps (as she calls my Instruments) if I do not make some profitable Use of them for the good of my Family. The Printer has offer'd me some considerable share of the Profits, and I have thus begun to comply with my Dame's desire.

The Argentine National Poultry and Rabbit Inspector's Almanac of Facts and Fictions, 1946

THE AREAS OF MY EXPERTISE

GOOD EVENING

My name is John Hodgman. I am not using a pseudonym.

As you may know, I was once a PROFESSIONAL LITERARY AGENT and high-powered media insider. In my day, I represented some of the finest young writers of our time, negotiating the sale of their books to publishers as well as their translation rights, screen rights, mustache fees, and bobblehead figurines. For this, I would receive a 15 percent commission, which is entirely standard, except for the bobblehead figurines, for which I received a 100 percent commission, because I carved the figurines myself, and my clients did not know that they existed. This is also entirely standard and should not be questioned.

But that is all over now. As it is our common destiny to become that which we most loathe, so I have become that most wretched and predictable thing, a PROFESSIONAL WRITER.

Normally I write short articles for magazines, which I find pleasing, as the process is usually over fairly quickly for both of us.

But now I have gone and written a book. Believe me, this was the last thing I wanted to do and, I suspect, the last thing you wanted as well. But I think we both knew it was inevitable. Certainly my publisher felt that it was, frequently pointing to my contract and its damned Inevitability Clause, which I should never have agreed to. But I did, and so now here we are.

I say "good evening," though of course I don't know what time it is where you are. This is one of the defining sorrows of books: that we cannot see each other. Of course it might have been different had my Publisher inserted the camera I designed to fit snugly in the spine of this book in order to spy on you. But this was determined to be "too expensive" and "too illegal," and so we are left once again to our imaginations.

The image I conjure of you, dear reader, begins with this book. For if you are reading these words, chances are you are probably reading this book, or one so similar to it that it doesn't matter. Moreover, I may presume you are holding this book with your own hands, or possibly mechanical hands that replaced your own hands after a terrible accident.

If I am correct, I may move on to deduce that you are a man or a woman. You are likely a person who has had some schooling—perhaps some training, for example, in *reading*. What's more, if you are reading this book, you are probably near some kind of light source. Unless this is the Braille edition of this book, you have use of at least one of your eyes. But I suspect you probably wear glasses, for people who read one book often go on to read another one, and then more and more—each longer than the last, and printed in increasingly painful fonts.

Finally, I may conclude that you are a curious person who thirsts for knowledge, for this is in fact a compendium of COMPLETE WORLD KNOWLEDGE. Here you shall find the answers to all of the questions you have been asking.

For example, you ask, "What is the truth about the Loch Ness monster?"

THE ANSWER IS PROVIDED.

You ask, "Who were the U.S. presidents who had hooks for hands?"

THE ANSWER IS PROVIDED.

"What was the menu at the first Thanksgiving," you ask, "and did it include eels?"

Technically, that is two questions, but do not apologize, for I shall answer them both . . . LATER.

Like all, you wonder, "What will happen in the future?"

A SIMPLE CHART OF OMENS AND PORTENTS PROVIDES THE ANSWER, and I am the author of that chart.

Of course, there have been books before this one dealing with monsters and eels and history and the future. I am indebted to the long history of the primer and the reader, the cyclopedia and the almanac.

Since ancient times, almanackers sought the future from the stars and from animal entrails, forecasting the weather, the tides, and the phases of the moon. This was valuable work, of course, though really only useful to farmers and sailors and werewolves.

It was Benjamin Franklin who realized that the form could offer more than just questionable meteorology. And so his *Poor Richard's Almanack* provided as well poetry, brief essays, and all kinds of unasked-for advice about when to wake up in the morning and how to electrocute yourself using only a kite and a pair of bifocals. I confess I am not a fan of this work, as Franklin seems to have been pretty sloppy, accidentally putting in Fs for every S. And you will note he *did* use a pseudonym, so it is difficult to trust him.

But even so, *Poor Richard* was exceedingly popular, and so the way was paved for a whole new genre of inexpensive popular reference books (*The North American Almanac, The World of Wisdom, The Old Werewolf's Almanack and Cyclopedia,* to name a few) offering history and wisdom and guidance on diverse subjects well into the last century. It was not long ago that the average American home kept only two books: an almanac and a Bible. Or else two almanacs (with one usually hidden in the wall to ward off ghosts). For they were an amazing innovation. At a time when most books were still intended only for scholars and aristocrats, often specifically fashioned to be held by foppish, consumptive hands, here was a book for the average person. Here at last was a place where the typical, lonely, miserable American could turn for the information he required on the lives of the vice presidents, the diseases of the horse, the rules of polite correspondence, the time required to digest certain foods and, naturally, on hoboes—all gathered together in brief, easy-to-read articles, all ingeniously arranged in no particular order whatsoever.

But as inspiring as these books were to me, I think you will agree that mine is a new kind of almanac and handy desk reference. For none before it has condensed so much information into such a pleasant, compact, and easily concealed *non-pseudonymous* volume, and none has focused so single-mindedly on THE AREAS OF MY EXPERTISE, with such extensive illuminating commentary by me.

On this point, I appreciate that it may be difficult to grasp how COMPLETE WORLD KNOWLEDGE may be contained within a single book. Some skeptics have pointed out that most libraries, for example, are physically larger than this book,[1] and thus must contain MORE KNOWLEDGE. This seems logical, but I wish to point out . . .

FIRST, many libraries contain *several copies of the same book*, not to mention large areas of *empty* space called "reading rooms" where the children and the vagrants and the freelance magazine writers meet. This book is considerably more compact and contains no rooms for vagrants.

SECOND, many libraries contain not only books of knowledge, but also a great number of novels. This is fine, but many novels, historically, are *longer than they need to be* and contain long sections that convey no knowledge. This is a structural matter more than anything else. Because books are assembled of equal-sized batches of folded pages called "signatures," there are often more pages than required by the words. Thence arose the practice of "padding" a novel, named for the eighteenth-century custom of physically upholstering the pages with velvet and horsehair in order to make a short book appear longer. This practice was discontinued when the vagrants found out about it, and it became common to open a novel and dis-

---

1. Though not all: please see "Two Libraries That Are Smaller Than This Book," p. 53.

cover a vagrant sleeping inside it. Instead, modern novelists now extend their works by including unnecessary additional words to the manuscript, sometimes at random, but more commonly in the form of long descriptions of cities and eyebrows and feelings.

THIRD, please note that when I say "vagrant," I am not talking about the unfortunate homeless souls who do not choose that life, but those few *willful wanderers* and *train-riding tricksters* who still believe the hobo wars are going on. Beware them, for these hobo emulators are often worse than the actual hoboes were themselves.

FOURTH, AND FINALLY, the main advantage that this book has over libraries, and indeed all of its almanackian predecessors, is that all of the historical oddities and amazing true facts contained herein are *lies, made up by me.* And it is this astonishing innovation that allows each entry to contain many more truths than if it were merely factual.

If this last point seems confusing to you, consider the banal and truthful statement that follows:

"Frederick Chopin was a Polish composer in the Romantic style who wrote primarily for the piano."

I guess this is sort of interesting, as most facts are. But history has shown us again and again that *facts are not what most humans believe.* They are not that which moves most men and women to love or hate or joy or crime.

Now COMPARE this statement:

"Frederick Chopin was a Polish composer in the Romantic style who was obsessed with ladybugs, often letting dozens of them gallop over his neck, arms, and long, tapering fingers while playing the piano."

Obviously the lie is so much more compelling. It shocks the mind and plays on the reader's imagination with ladybug-covered hands. New resonances emerge, and new melodies of insight, not just into the nature of Chopin, but also the art of composing, the history of the ladybug as a good-luck charm, and coleopteraphilia. It also finally explains how Chopin solved his terrible aphid problem.

Truth may be stranger than fiction, goes the old saw, but it is never as strange as lies. (Or, for that matter, as true.) Proof of which maxim is the fact that I just made it up.

Now, I sense that you have further questions. Such as "Would the hidden-camera system you proposed for this book have allowed me to see you, as well?" Obviously no. That would be offensive. But I admire suspicion, and you are reasonable to ponder who is this John Hodgman and how did he come to know so many invented facts?

As I write this, I am currently sitting on a very uncomfortable chair in my observatory on the Upper West Side of Manhattan, surrounded by books and cats. Mine is the typical life of the professional writer: one of quiet contemplation and knowledge-gathering and masturbation and the cashing of enormous checks. But I wish you to know that even though I have surrounded myself with books and draw from them the great consolation of literature (as well as protection from smaller-caliber bullets), I have not failed to live.

I have been a stock boy, a dishwasher, a radio disc jockey, a cheesemonger, and a traffic counter. I once was able to play the viola, and I was also a clarinetist (though the preferred term is "wood-winder"). I have traveled to at least seven states and several foreign countries. This includes England where, on a charge of "leaning an object against the fence" (police code for nighttime drunken zoo-invasion), I spent a night in a London jail, which my captors insisted on spelling "G-A-O-L." This is but one of the ways they tortured me. Let us not speak of it again.

Later, being a literary agent offered me insight into the world of publishing, which I share at length in this work. And later still, as I have plied my modest trade as a professional writer, so have I become as well an expert in lobster rolls, the economy of malls, rural Sardinia, wing-tip shoes, the history of comic books, the legality of sword canes, "fat pants," and most other subjects, including the subject of COMPLETE WORLD KNOWLEDGE.

This is the gift I want to share with you, dear reader—the one I hardly deserve myself. And by avoiding things like "plots" and "themes" and "complete sentences," I hope to repay your time with a very useful book that you will turn to many times in your life, I hope buying a new copy each time.

This book was not written with any special equipment besides the English language and a standard Sentence Machine. I should say that despite my vast, innate reserves of knowledge I did perform some research in the preparation of this book—but I promise you it was scant, haphazard, and largely accidental. Still I suppose it's possible that a few actual facts may have slipped through to these pages, and for this I apologize. If you discover any of these errors, you may of course write[2] and we will attempt to correct the matter in future editions.

But if I guess correctly, you are not the sort of person who is obsessed with writing annoying little letters, and for this, I congratulate you. If I am not wrong, you are a smart, open-minded person who probably does not have mechanical hands. As you use your normal, organic, nonmechanical hands to leaf through the pages of this book, I am guessing you will gradually come to a better understanding of the world we share—perhaps not the world exactly as it is today, but as it might become someday, if I have my way. And if I am not wrong, you may now look out the window and see that it is evening. And so to you I can only say thank you, welcome, and good evening.

That is all.

---

2. P.O. Box 1618 Cathedral Station, New York NY, 10025.

A NOTE ON ORGANIZATION

I wish to reassure the modern reader that this book meets your requirements. It is composed of 55 discrete articles, tables, and figures, and, like almanacs and experimental Latin American novels of old, you are encouraged to read them in any order, skipping them as you please, and following narrative threads of your own weaving. The footnotes will only point out the most obvious thematic echoes and authorial redundancies.

That said, all effort has also been made to provide a satisfying experience to the old-fashioned reader who chooses to read from start to finish. For example, the pages have been ingeniously numbered in the order in which they appear, and they have also been fashioned out of light paper for easy turning by frail hands. Good luck, old-timer. I hope you enjoy yourself.

A NOTE ON SPORTS

Please note that there are only two references to sports in this book. They are on pages 71 and 95, and both are appropriately dismissive. If you wish for sports information, might I kindly refer you to every other aspect of our culture?

TABLE OF CONTENTS

WHAT WILL HAPPEN IN THE FUTURE

INFORMATION YOU WILL FIND USEFUL IN THE PRESENT

CONTENTS CONTINUES

WHAT YOU DID NOT KNOW ABOUT THE PAST

WHAT YOU DID NOT KNOW ABOUT HOBOES

FURTHER INFORMATION YOU CAN USE TODAY

OUR 51 UNITED STATES

THERE IS MORE PAST THAN YOU THOUGHT

GOOD MORNING — 223

A SPECIAL BONUS EXCERPT
FROM MY NEXT BOOK — 224

TABLE OF TABLES

CONTENTS CONTINUES

TABLE OF FIGURES

PART ONE

WHAT WILL HAPPEN
IN THE FUTURE

LYCANTHROPIC TRANSFORMATION TIMETABLES			
FIRST SEVENTH			
	MINUTES AFTER MOONRISE/MOONSET		
	to-Wolf	to-Man	Transformation
Werewolf (North American)	14'21"	12'24"	wolfish mood
Hombre Lobo	12'32"	10'24"	claws, whisker stumps
Werewolf (British)	13'43"	43'12"	rudimentary tail
Loup-Garou	29'00"	24'02"	howling
Varcolac	42'12"	21'21"	keen sight, smell
Libahunt	32'31"	24'29"	wolfish voice
Werebears and Skinwalkers	no effect	no effect	none

CHARM POTENCY	
silver items	high
wolfsbane	moderate/high
fur girdle removal	effective
taming love of pure woman	modest

OMENS AND PORTENTS FOR THE COMING YEAR

Traditional almanacs regularly included information about what to expect in the coming year with regard to crop yields, tidal patterns, moonrises, and so on. However, they were hardly scientific, relying heavily on astrology and various ancient methods of "scrying," such as crystal gazing, tea-leaf reading, sheepdog consultation, and guessing.

But modern times require modern methods, and also more general predictions for those who are not necessarily farmers or sailors[3] or werewolves. Thus, the accompanying OMENS V. PORTENTS table, of the kind currently in use by most actuaries.[4]

As these scientific soothsayers know, the signature of the future is written on the here and now. Thanks to careful observation and experimentation we now know, for example, that a rise in oil prices occurring in the same year as the birth of an albino buffalo will cause us to inevitably embrace polygamy and the open use of jet packs.

Herewith some more commonly observed predictors that, when correlated, produce some of the more startling predictions for the coming year.

FIGURE 1: *Omen Tabulation Pool, Circa 1989*

---

3. Actually, some deference is still made here to sailors. Those salty fellows may read on to "Special Long-Term Predictions for Sailors," p. 35, if they are indeed capable of reading at all.

4. For more information on actuaries, their customs, and their tattoos, please see "On Actuaries and Their Tattoos," p. 37.

TABLE 1: OMENS V. PORTENTS

PORTENTS OBSERVED OMENS OBSERVED*	} *Jormungand the serpent rising from the deep to fill the skies with venom*	*A cat consorts with a skunk.*	
A wooly bear caterpillar crossing the road	So-called "altruism" will be abandoned in favor of a new policy of enlightened self-interest and orgies.	Mankind will learn to communicate with cheese.	
A broken gravestone	All humans will speak a common wordless click language called "mmntk!mmm!"	Humans born with prehensile tails will no longer be immediately drafted into the secret army but allowed to live a normal life; they will, however, be declawed.	
An obese boy eating corn on the cob	Most white-collar workers will parachute to work.	In-brain television becomes a reality.	
A car that keeps going even after the needle has long passed "Empty"	An alien consciousness will offer earth a "miracle drug" via electronic mail.	Fully carpeted space liners take tourists to the pleasure satellites.	
Someone speaking in an obviously affected accent	Everyone will wear very tight, clingy shirts.	Ragnarok**	
Death of the Norse god Balder	Ragnarok**	Solar flares will cause a dimensional shift such that all humans will dress and talk like gangsters from Chicago circa 1930.	
* See Notes, page 34.	** See Notes, page 34.		

TABLE 1: OMENS V. PORTENTS *continued*

A sea urchin arrives in the mail with no return address	*Canadian quarters and/or hobo nickels given as change in the United States*	*An owl that screeches with the voice of a man*	*A picture of a cyclops (or an actual cyclops)*
Perpetual night will cause an increase in sale of enormous fur coats.	Most housework will be performed by a combination of microscopic robots and astral projection.	Mankind will be united in worshipping a single sentient computer named Doublebrain.	Ragnarok**
Food pellets will cause the growth of gigantic children who will be used to sweep the gigantic chimneys at the food pellet factory.	Electric scooters will replace congressmen.	Ragnarok**	Only three "corporate nations" will continue to exist, each owned by a brand of energy drink.
Merman attacks on the transatlantic, suboceanic tunnel will increase.	Ragnarok**	Most Americans will get their news from an inter-connected tele-dial service. "Tloggers" call your house several times a day giving you their take on world events.	Genetically advanced chimpanzee clones will be trained to communicate with quantum computers.
Ragnarok**	Everyone will have a cotton candy machine installed in his or her car.	Grapes will be delicious and not disgusting.	Roving cocktail gangs will ravage American cities in search of vermouth.
Cancer will be cured using a combination of traditional herbs and innovative new poultices.	Wearable computers will be commonplace and will feature sporty epaulets.	All homes will be connected by pneumatic tubes filled with mice.	Dozens of 1940s-era battleships that were "timeshifted" in secret govern-ment experiments appear in a child's glass of milk.
Dinosaurs will return from space on their giant comet with a message for the mammals.	Every American city will be covered in sparkly dust that shall make it seem like a dream.	Dentists will be mobilized to deal with the problem of human fangs.	A pirate fashion craze will inspire thousands of American teen-agers to cut off their own legs and replace them with wooden pegs.

FIGURE 2: *An Ominous Portent*

*Omens and Portents must be observed in the same three-month period. If a sword or picture of a sword is observed the same day, the omen and/or portent must be discarded from consideration. If you are a sailor or seaman, please see "Special Long-Term Predictions for Sailors" on page 35.

**This is an actuarial term that should not be confused with the more popularly understood definition from Norse mythology. In those epic sagas, "Ragnarok" referred to the predestined end of the world, in which the gods known as the Aesir will meet the legions of evil led by Loki, the trickster god, on the battlefield of Vigrid—a doomed confrontation in which nearly all participants will perish and the earth itself will be consumed in fire. Among professional actuaries, however (at least those who are not Vikings), "Ragnarok" refers to the same event, but it is not believed that Surt will join the battle with his army of fire giants, and most of the Aesir will die instead from lifestyle-related causes long after the battle itself, including smoking, snuff-taking, and mead-addiction. In both cases, however, all humans die in flame.

TABLE 2: SPECIAL LONG-TERM PREDICTIONS FOR SAILORS

Omen	24 hours	7 days	1 year	25 years	50 years	75 years	100 years
Red sky at morning	Sailors take warning.	Sailors start to feel like they can do nothing right.	Sailors mistreat their wives, believing they do not deserve love.	Sailors fear the sea, loathe the land, and frequently call the sky an ass.	Sailors tie weights around their sunken chests and toss themselves into the sea, briefly glimpsing a luminous underwater city before their lungs are finally choked with brine.	Sailors' bones are used as flutes by the pitiless mermen.	Ragnarok**
Red sky at night	Sailors' delight.	Sailors dance a happy jig.	Sailors' dancing becomes prideful, reckless.	Sailors fall off deck and are rescued by strange, blue-skinned humanoids with fish tails.	Sailors can breathe underwater, but are kept by the mermen as playthings in their city of barnacle buildings and luminous algae lights.	Sailors cursed by merman magic to immortality pray for death in underwater zoo.	Ragnarok**

FIG. 3: *Playthings of the Mermen*

ALTERNATE METHOD FOR PREDICTING THE FUTURE

On a clean square sheet of paper, neatly write . . .

> Your favorite color
> Your favorite appetizer
> Your favorite non-wine alcohol
> The name of the last person to cut your hair
> The name of the street you grew up on
> The name of your first pet
> Your porn name
> Your favorite method of telling the future

Assign each letter a number value based on its position in the alphabet (i.e., A=1, M=13, AA=27, etc.). Add the number values of the first letter and last letter of each item on the list. Write that number down at the bottom of the sheet.

Fold the sheet of paper in half, corner to corner, to form two triangles. Unfold it, and then fold it again, this time joining the opposite corners. Now fold it into a paper balloon in the traditional manner.

If you have done it correctly, there should be a little opening at the top of the balloon. Whisper a secret into this hole. Then light a match and drop it into the balloon, covering the top with your thumb such that the fire consumes all the air in the balloon along with your secret and then goes out.

Then set the balloon on fire in the traditional manner and collect the ashes. Carefully put the ashes into an envelope, add a self-addressed stamped envelope, seal it, and mail it "first class" to the following address:

P.O. BOX x

James A. Farley Post Office 441

NYC, NY 10001

In which x is the number you tabulated on your sheet of paper before you burned it.

In 3–7 weeks, you shall receive a letter bearing the name of the person you are going to marry.

(Hint: it's not Tim.)

(Note: If you do not remember the number you tabulated on your sheet of paper before you burned it, you will never marry.)

(Note: If you receive no reply, DO NOT go to the post office and stake out the P.O. boxes, for this is not a mystery you can solve, and also you will eventually be arrested.)

ON ACTUARIES AND THEIR TATTOOS

Some summers ago, I had lunch with a famous movie director in his hometown of Omaha, Nebraska. As he showed me around, the July sun got high and hot, and so we took shelter in Johnny's Café, a dark cavern of a steakhouse in the center of the old stockyards. It was so powerfully air-conditioned inside that the generously padded, fake leather swivel chairs felt like they had spent the night in the refrigerator, and we sat there, sunblind, awaiting our onion rings.

It was quiet. The only other party sat at a large, round table nearby: eight men, the youngest perhaps thirty-nine, the oldest in his sixties, all pleased and prosperous-seeming, all eating the prime rib special, one sprinkling sugar on top of it. They had draped their jackets over their chairs, and they wore short-sleeved dress shirts. This allowed me to observe that they all, in fact, had tattoos, each about the same size, on the inside of their forearms.

"They are actuaries," explained the movie director when I directed his attention to this odd coincidence.

The city, as you know, was named for the Omaha people, whose leader Big Elk once said, "Death will come, always out of season." Omaha is a beef town and a Warren Buffett town (if you wish to find his modest home in Robin Hood Hills, just stand on any street corner, put a quarter on its side, and it will roll there). And Omaha is an insurance town, drawing actuaries from all over the world to read mortality tables and stochastic models and divine from them the hard fortunes of our lives and the seasons of our deaths.

The actuaries, said the movie director, are not trained within a company but are hired from one of several international guilds. And a large insurance company will often hire several actuaries from different guilds to perform the same function, as each guild has its own method and outlook. Some are more optimistic, whereas others are notoriously grim (one rogue guild, the Actuarial Society of Transylvania, routinely claims that any child who lives to the age of fifteen without becoming a werewolf is an unaccountable anomaly). And each guild has its own tattoo.

Here are those tattoos I observed that afternoon at Johnny's:

—A crystal ball: Casualty Actuarial Society, est. 1917, Arlington, Va., headquarters.

—An empty teacup: The Society of Actuaries, est. 1949, Schaumburg, Ill., headquarters.

—A sheep's entrails: International Actuarial Association, est. 1895, Ottowa, Ont., headquarters.

—A man hanging by his ankles: Danish Society of Actuaries, est. 1901, Copenhagen, Denmark, headquarters.

—A snake eating its own tail at a predictable rate: Faculty and Institute of Actuaries, est. 1848, Edinburgh and London, dual headquarters.

—The actuarial notation l_x, meaning the number of people alive at age x: American Academy of Actuaries, est. 1965, Washington, D.C., headquarters.

—A complete but very small ouija board: Royal Association of Belgian Actuaries, est. 1895, Brussels, headquarters.

—A child werewolf: The Actuarial Society of Transylvania, est. 1973, Indianapolis, Ind., headquarters (no actual connection to Transylvania).[5]

The men at the table near me were all from different guilds, but they were perfectly collegial, talking in the warm and hearty tones of satisfied men who share a respected profession that also connects them to a kind of elite worldwide fraternity.

"No one makes movies about guys like this," the movie director now said softly, with a kind of sadness. "Just ordinary Americans sitting around predicting the future."

Our lunch arrived, and we ate. I don't mind saying: the onion rings were amazing. But then a surprising thing happened. The other table grew quiet. One by one, each actuary raised his glass of Diet Sprite to one of their fellows, a sandy-haired, round-faced man in his fifties—the one with the hanged-man tattoo. Each man silently drained his glass, replacing it on the table upside down. Then, one by one, they left the table, leaving the man alone.

There are some things that are forbidden among all the actuarial guilds, I later learned, though they are difficult to resist. The sandy-haired man had predicted the exact date and time of his own death, a power that each actuary possesses but is encouraged not to use, for it tends to color all his future analysis darkly. The ritual we observed was, in effect, his excommunication from the company of the actuaries of Omaha. If he were lucky, I learned, he might start over again elsewhere, perhaps in Hartford, Connecticut. But he would be, as you might imagine, forever haunted by what he had learned.

"You see," the movie director said, "our cinema should reflect this!

---

5. I found out all these details later from an actuarial Web site, as well as the interesting fact that novelty shops sometimes sell wooden or plastic tiles with these images printed upon them. You cast them in the air and by their arrangement as they fall, you can read your fate, or so claims the packaging. Professional actuaries, however, frown on this practice, even when it proves accurate.

As Big Elk said, 'Misfortunes do not flourish particularly in our lives—they grow everywhere.'"

Which, of course, is why Big Elk is called "the First Actuary."

The movie director no longer lives in Omaha, and neither does the sandy-haired man. I like to imagine that these two outcasts' lives may intertwine again someday, but chances of this, I know, are slim.

PART TWO

INFORMATION
YOU WILL FIND USEFUL
IN THE PRESENT

LYCANTHROPIC TRANSFORMATION TIMETABLES			
SECOND SEVENTH			
	MINUTES AFTER MOONRISE/MOONSET		
	to-Wolf	to-Man	Transformation
Werewolf (North American)	10'21"	12'24"	stooping, slathering
Hombre Lobo	9'34"	10'24"	fine fur
Werewolf (British)	8'21"	43'12"	jaws/claws
Loup–Garou	6'29"	24'02"	flesh–thirst, leaping
Varcolac	8'20"	21'21"	contempt for humans
Libahunt	12'31"	24'29"	fine fur, yellow eyes
Werebears and Skinwalkers	58'23"	29'34"	only anger

CHARM POTENCY		
silver items	moderate/high	
wolfsbane	waxing	
fur girdle removal	50% effect	
taming love of pure woman	waning	

ACTIVE

HOW TO WRITE A BOOK:
THE FIFTY-FIVE DRAMATIC SITUATIONS

Here is something true that I have long observed regarding people who have written books: Their clothes fit well. They seem relaxed and happy, as if they are thinking, Well, at least I got that done. At least I wrote a book. They are not anxiety-ridden, badly tailored nervous wrecks like me, for example, or all of you. That is why so many people want to write books, and when I finish writing this book, perhaps my clothes will fit better too.

And so you may be wondering, "Apart from an almanac of COM-PLETE WORLD KNOWLEDGE, which I recognize as being your original idea and an enforceable copyright, what is the best kind of book to write?"

I was asked this many times when I was a professional literary agent. The answer at that time was obvious: The most *marketable* kind of book to write was one in which vampires fight serial killers. But the *best* kind of book was one in which the vampires fight large weather systems and perfect storms.

Of course, that answer isn't correct in today's publishing environment, as neither sort of those examples includes a worldwide conspiracy overseen by a centuries-old religious secret society. While my initial response dates me hopelessly, literature—bless it—ever grows and matures.

But though the particulars may change, I think it is certainly safe to say that throughout history all effective stories are based in some sort of conflict.

And most critics agree that in literature, there are five primal conflicts. These are:

—Man versus man
—Man versus nature
—Man versus society
—Man versus himself
—Man versus cyborgs

If you imagine a story, any story, I trust you will find that it will fit neatly into one of these rubrics. But do not panic. You should feel no need to actually imagine a story. History has already done the work for you, as this table of dramatic situations, organized by type of conflict, shall prove.

FIGURE 4: *Typical Cyborg Mischief*

TABLE 3: THE FIFTY-FIVE DRAMATIC SITUATIONS

Man/Woman v. Man/Woman	Man/Woman v. Nature	Man/Woman v. Society	Man/Woman v. Him-/Herself	Man/Woman v. Cyborgs
Boy v. Girl	Mountains thwart progress.	A stranger comes to town.	Triumph over ennui	Threat of cyborgs from the future
Cop v. Rookie	Zoo animals attack zookeepers.	A town springs up magically around a stranger.	Success thwarted by phobia	Threat of present-day cyborgs
Magicians v. Detectives	All animals attack all humans.*	Society persecutes inventor of revolutionary fabric or vehicle.	Hero must choose between excellent sexual partner and stable companion.	Return of Civil War–era cyborgs that are powered by steam
Teacher v. Unruly class; both learn lessons.	Hunted by tornadoes	Self-satisfied loner flouts irrational laws, reveals absurdity of society, congratulates himself.	Past life reasserts itself.	Cyborg fights the man within.
Pursuit throughout life by a French constable whose determination exceeds his reason	Volcanoes come to town.	Hero is chased by townspeople bearing torches.	Hero wonders if closest friend is actually his archenemy, then lives in fear.	Man seeks control of his own cybernetic brain.
Country mouse v. City mouse	One partially blinded by bear seeks revenge.	Person living in two-dimensional world encourages embrace of third dimension and is shunned.	A horrible physical deformity is overcome, only to be revealed that it is all in the protagonist's imagination.	Only the hero can see the cyborgs who secretly run our government and media.

* Please see page 46.

TABLE 3: THE FIFTY-FIVE DRAMATIC SITUATIONS *continued*

Man/Woman v. Man/Woman	Man/Woman v. Nature	Man/Woman v. Society	Man/Woman v. Him-/Herself	Man/Woman v. Cyborgs
Devil worshippers v. Apartment dwellers	Wilderness becomes crucible in which asthmatic learns to grow a beard.	Conscience prevents acceptance of Soylent Green.	One partially blinded by bear overcomes need for revenge.	Family pet discovered to be cyborg.
Rivals in business become partners in bed.	The ocean arrives to put an end to well-laid plans.	True talent overlooked in favor of kiss-asses.	Struggle to overcome the effects of brainwashing/hypnosis	Young, handsome cyborg Army officer kills his own family, blames hippies.
Former lovers who are archeologists seek same ancient curio.	Petty jealousy inspires tireless pursuit of whale.	New numbering system for clones proves problematic for non-clones.	Everything turns out to be a dream.	Man creates cyborg who wishes to be a real boy.
Evil cousins thwart romance.	Saint Bernards come first as rescuers, then reveal themselves as enemies.	Shark loves Jet (also can be Man v. Nature or Nature v. Technology).	Body part is severed, gains mind of its own: Watch out.	Cyborg servants turn on master.
Professional debunker v. Popular spoon-bending psychic	Snakes lie in wait.	Child raised by Saint Bernard assassins seeks acceptance and forgive-ness of human society.	Hero in coma seeks to solve his own murder, discovers culprit is himself.	Cyborgs seek fortune on Broadway, settle for bartending gig, and learn much about human life.

A CLARIFICATION REGARDING THE DRAMATIC
SITUATION IN WHICH HUMANS FIGHT ANIMALS

I wish to clarify here that I am not against the animals. I have two cats, and they are very amusing. I have a particular fondness for those quasi-mammals called the monotremes—the duckbilled platypus, the spiny anteater, and their ilk—because they have beaks instead of teeth, and no external ears, and milk glands without nipples, and you have to admit that takes some gumption. Generally speaking, I think it is fair to say that I am a friend to the creatures of the earth when I am not busy eating them or wearing them.

But recently I found myself once again at three in the morning cleaning up one of my cats' vomit, moving swiftly of course, so that the other cat would not swoop in and eat it.[6] And at that moment, I confess I felt in my heart a certain measure of ambivalence about this relationship.

This feeling came up again recently when I was talking with a colleague about the monkeys that help people in wheelchairs by answering their phones and brushing their teeth and writing all their thank-you notes. This is, on its face, a noble thing to do. But I wondered: why are they only helping people in wheelchairs?

At best, the monkeys are being stingy. But at worst, they may have a more nefarious plan in mind. Perhaps they are choosing the weakest members of our herd on purpose. We all know from the movie *Monkey Shines* that your average capuchin is but a single super-brain injection away from turning into a razor-wielding killing machine. Just as we all know from *The Birds* that the mere sight of Tippi Hedren in a boat, bringing all her big-city sexiness to chaste Bodega Bay, will drive all the birds in northern California (what else but) apeshit crazy.

The person who wants to make a million dollars, I have long maintained, could of course do so very easily by crafting a script or a novel

---

6. Please see "Common Short and Long Cons," p. 148.

based on this elemental premise: ALL ANIMALS V. ALL HUMANS. I trust you feel the immediate, primal clutch of this concept on your heart, and I can promise you that the duckbilled platypus scene alone will be worth the price of admission.

MORE MATTERS LITERARY: THE SIX ESSENTIALS

Even once you have chosen a Dramatic Situation, however, writing a book can still be a tedious process. According to my own observation, every writer must have six essentials at his command. Some are born with them. Others must develop them over many years, or hire a professional to provide them.[7] They are . . .

1. empathy
2. the willingness to endure solitude
3. the belief that the world cares about what you have to say
4. the ability to describe facial hair accurately
5. a large desk in a quiet room of your own in which to chase your demons (preferably a circular room, so that the demons have no place to hide)
6. special stationery with pictures of typewriters and/or quills on top

FIGURE 5: *Can You Describe Capt. Thompson's Facial Hair?*

7. This is most common for "empathy," and it is not unusual for even the finest novelists to hire a ghost empathizer for their third or fourth book.

WHEN WRITING, PLEASE AVOID
THESE FAILED PALINDROMES

Slow speed: deep owls

Drat That Tard

Two Owls Hoot Who Owls Hoot Too (Owt)

Sour candy and Dan C. Roused

Desire still lisps: Arise! D.

A man, a plan, a kind of man-made river, planned.

Hobos! So!

Eh, S'occurs to Me to Succor She

Tow a What? Thaw!

FIGURE 6: *Deep Owls*

WERE YOU AWARE OF IT?

This is the first of several examples from my newspaper column of the same name that ran every Sunday, right under *Prince Valiant,* in the *New York Times* for twenty-eight years. The original columns contained wonderful illustrations by Charles "Sparky" Schulz, whom you may recall as the creator of *Snoopy & Dilbert.* But as I do not control the rights to Sparky's spot drawings (and most of the time they were just pictures of men with extremely long fingernails anyway and had nothing to do with the subject at hand), I do not include them here.

Tennyson wrote, "It is the height of luxury to sit in a hot bath and read about little birds."

    I'm sure you are glad to know Tennyson's bathing habits. But were you aware that . . .

—Robert Frost bathed by rolling around in the Vermont dust once a year?

—Wallace Stevens showered in beer?

—Homer allowed others to bathe him, but because he was blind, he could not tell that they were just *pretending* to bathe him?

—Emily Dickinson collected little soaps?

—Guillaume Apollinaire shaved himself with a photograph of a razor that had been fitted with a razor's edge?

WERE YOU AWARE OF IT!?!

WHERE TO SELL YOUR SHORT STORIES

Some people are too lazy to write whole novels, and so they devote their time to short fiction or books of lists. I cannot speak to the market for the latter, but anyone who is telling you there isn't a market for serious short fiction anymore is certainly not me. Indeed, many popular magazines are very eager to buy your short stories, especially if your short stories are written in the form of twenty-five-word raunchy photo captions.

TABLE 4: WHERE TO MARKET YOUR STORIES THAT SOUND EXACTLY LIKE RAUNCHY PHOTO CAPTIONS

Maxim

FHM

Stuff

Gear

Things To Purchase Or Masturbate To

Harper's

If this is not your natural milieu as a writer, however, there are still a few respectable magazines out there devoted to publishing short stories in the classic genres. For example . . .

TABLE 5: OTHER MARKETS FOR YOUR SHORT STORIES	
Where to Market Your Short Stories About Life and Death At High Altitudes	*Crossbow!* *Icecutter: A Magazine For Men* *Fisticuff* *Male Journey*
Where to Market Your Short Stories About Life and Death On the Sea or Beneath It	*Compound Crossbow!* *False Sea Tales* *Destination: Endanger* *Outdare!*
Where to Market Your Short Stories About Erotic Encounters in Either of the Above Locales	*Sexy Peril* *Secret Sunburn* *Spicy Brine* *Yankee*
Where to Market Your Alternate-History Short Stories	*The New Amsterdamer* *The Pacific Monthly* *The Paris Review* *Red Dawn* *Colony 51: The Magazine That Dares to Imagine What Would Happen If the Roswell Crash Had Occurred in 1679* *The Ottower—The National Magazine of Fiction and Comment for All Crown Subjects of the United States . . . Of Canada!*
Where to Market Your Short Stories Featuring Lots of Footnotes, Comic Book References, and Lists	(8)
Where to Market Your Charles Bukowski/Raymond Carver Slash Fiction	*Penthouse,* circa 1981 *What We Talk About When We Talk About Raymond Carver Having Sex with Charles Bukowski Monthly*

8. "The Journal for Extra Smart Boys"

IDIOSYNCRASIES OF THE GREAT DETECTIVES

—Miss Millicent McTeague: This elderly spinster is not as senile as she seems! Also, she eats cats.

—Juno Dix: This refined, morbidly obese attorney solves mysteries without ever leaving his own bathtub.

—Inspector Franz Duvet-Perez: This fastidious foreigner refuses to say exactly what country he is from, thus keeping everyone guessing.

—Buddy Jimmy Smith: This freckle-faced fourth-grader is actually the reincarnation of an Egyptian slave whose ancient memories of embalming techniques mystically guide him as he cracks "The Case of Janey's Kitten, Who Has Been Missing for Days."

—Brother Metrigon: This tenth-century monk actually believes he is a ninth-century monk.

—Sergeant Demonicus Rex: This uniformed police officer is also a high magus in the Church of Satan.

—Dr. Kathleen DiPietro: This brilliant forensic medical examiner occasionally wears the victims' skin in order to "see the crime through their eyes." This habit becomes something of a liability when she begins wearing the victims' skin to nightclubs and restaurants.

—Lord Miles Overstreet: This debonair, mentally ill aristocrat does not realize that he is his own nemesis, the mad Dr. Craig Kittles.[9]

---

9. A prime example of the dramatic situation known as "Man v. Himself," as per "How to Write a Book: The Fifty-Five Dramatic Situations," p. 42.

TWO LIBRARIES THAT ARE SMALLER
THAN THIS BOOK

THE STERLING MEMORIAL LIBRARY,
YALE UNIVERSITY, 2ND REGRESSION

Atop Yale University's imposing Sterling Memorial Library the curious will find something incredible: air-conditioning vents, and also, a complete model of the great walled city of New Haven made of copper. It is very detailed and includes all the buildings of Yale University. A waist-high Sterling Memorial Library stands at its center, and atop that there is yet another perfect model of New Haven, containing yet another Sterling, and so on, into infinity. This second Sterling Memorial Library (which, by the way, is the nation's third-largest Sterling Memorial Library) is designed to hold a single volume, which contains within its pages the fate of the United States, in great detail, through the year 3000.[10]

THE HALLELUJAH MAN COLLECTION

In a small binder hidden behind garbage cans on Columbus Avenue and 106th Street in New York City are collected all of the small religious booklets that have been distributed by the "Hallelujah Man," a handsome, elderly West Indian gentleman who walks the neighboring streets shouting "Hallelujah" every day until he grows too hoarse to continue.

HANDY MEASUREMENTS OF TIME
WHEN YOU DO NOT HAVE A WATCH

Before it was common to wear a wristwatch, Americans had to either purchase the correct time at a time parlor or, if they lived in a rural area, wait until the time peddler came to town. After some haggling,

---

10. Please see "Secrets of Yale University," p. 143.

the agreed price would be paid, and then the peddler would draw a black curtain back to reveal a clock. Those who could not afford this luxury relied instead on simple folk wisdom, deriving these methods of time approximation that you may still find useful.

—It takes exactly five seconds to read this sentence aloud.

— Find a cesium-133 atom. It will take exactly one half hour for it to oscillate between the two hyperfine levels of its ground state 16,546,737,186,000 times. Most car dashboards now come equipped with a cesium-133 atom for just this purpose.

— A certified speed-reader will be able to read this entire book in exactly an hour. Certified speed-readers may be contracted in the county clerk's office.

— Using only the stones and twigs around you, it will take you exactly 120 minutes to construct a working sundial.

— When you realize you should have simply apologized, it will be exactly 11:50 P.M. Needless to say: too late.

— When driving at night, the ghostly hitchhiker will reappear on the side of the road exactly once per hour, for exactly four hours, before giving up.

— A "fortnight martini," when properly made, will not reach room temperature for fourteen days.

— If you do not meet them a second time, you will forget the name and face of everyone you meet within five years.

— The agave or "century" plant will live for 100 years. Caution: At year 100, it will come alive and devour the person closest to it.

TABLE 6: TIPPING GUIDE TO THE GREAT HOTELS: TO INSURE PROMPT SERVICE

Doorman	Tip $2–5 for unloading your luggage or hailing a cab.	Starling Boy	Tip $1 for chasing starlings from room.
Chambermaid	Tip $1–3 per day for room cleaning, turn-down service.	Porte-a-Merde	Tip $5 at night.[11]
Concierge	Tip $10–20 per day for aiding with social/business itinerary.	Sculptor	Tip $25 per bust of self.
Room Service	Gratuity added on bill, add 5% for exemplary service.	Blesser	Tip $5 for blessing the room and checking closets for the undead.
Lullaby Service	Tip $5 per lullaby. I cannot stress this enough: each lullaby deserves its own gratuity. Add $2 if the lullabulist uses a harp.	Jet-en-Mer	Tip $2–4 for tossing your ringing alarm clock out the window into the sea; add $4 for larger items or family members.
Phrenologist	Tip $5 per skull-fondling.	Melancholier	Tip $10 to have the melancholier help you stop laughing.
House Detective	Tip $20 per solved crime.	Feral Turn-Down Service	Tip $1–2 to have a bed made on the floor of leaves and dense grasses if you were raised by creatures in the wild.
Muralist	Tip $15 on top of hotel fee for a full-wall, color pastoral mural; $25 for a mural depicting the struggle of labor in the twentieth century; add an additional 10% for a trompe l'oeil.		
24-Hour Magician	Tip $20 for 40-minute routine; $30 if demon summoned.		

11. Due to indoor plumbing, it is unusual to find a dedicated porte-a-merde standing on call to spirit away "night soil" at any hour. However, for older guests, many hotels still provide this service, which generally falls to the Starling Boy.

FIGURE 7: *Prepare to Tip Extra for Demonic Summoning*

JOKES THAT HAVE NEVER PRODUCED LAUGHTER

Comedians are notoriously superstitious, more so even than actors, who fear the word "Macbeth" so much that they will attempt to stab anyone who dares speak or print it. This is why Shakespeare is dead now, and why I remain in hiding. Comedians, on the other hand, hate only themselves. That is why you will occasionally still hear these jokes, even though they supposedly curse the speaker to never hear laughter again. If you are hosting a dinner party or looking to pep up a speech to your coworkers, do not tell these jokes. I would also advise avoiding them in wedding toasts, retirement parties, eulogies, casual conversation, or joke books. Please note: the authors of these jokes are unknown. The earliest extant versions of them are kept in a vault at the Friar's Club in Los Angeles, in the same room where they keep Buddy Hackett's mummy.

1. A man goes into a bar. He has a dog with him. The dog is wearing an eye patch. The man says to the bartender, "Ask me about my dog." Unfortunately, the bartender does not hear him, because he went deaf in one ear as a child. He serves a woman at the other end of the bar. When he comes around to the man with the dog again, the man orders an imported beer. He forgets what he was going to say about the dog.

2. A priest, a rabbi, and a nonreligious person are flying across the Atlantic Ocean, all for different reasons. There is engine trouble, and one of the wings catches on fire. The plane starts to go down. Luckily, there are enough parachutes for everyone. Evacuation is orderly.

3. An Irishman, an Englishman, and an Indian chief go fishing together in a large rowboat in a medium-sized lake. Everyone has good luck: two or three big fish each. They stay out in the middle of the lake until sunset. On the way back to shore, as the sky purples and turns to night, they all sing a song.

4. A duck goes into a pharmacy. He says to the pharmacist, "I need some ointment for my beak. It is very chapped." The pharmacist says, "We have nothing for ducks here."

5. A dog goes into a bar. He is wearing an eye patch. The dog says to the bartender, "Have you heard the one about the one-eyed dog?" The bartender, who is deaf in one ear, thinks the dog is mak-

ing fun of him. He asks him to leave. The dog says, "Don't you have a sense of humor, deafie?" At the end of his shift, the bartender is tired of all the jokes. Today it's a one-eyed dog. Yesterday it was a horse with rickets. The day before: ants. He lives above the bar, in a small room. He spends the night alone there, listening to his battery-operated radio, which picks up only a bad jazz station. He listens to bad jazz with his bad ear.

GOVERNMENT PROGRAMS YOU CAN TAKE ADVANTAGE OF **TODAY**

I've done all the legwork! All you have to do is make the call!

$10,000 to teach yourself how to make a samurai sword!

$1,000 to become a French gendarme! (Cape fee included!)

$5,000 to build a garden shed out of floppy disks!

$20,000 to educate mink in your own home!

$250 to glue photographs of bees into a book!

$5,000 to wear spats and suspenders and ask the world to take you seriously!

$2,500 to crumple tinfoil and then smooth it out again!

$10,000 to open a portal to another dimension (void if dimension is inhabited by world-devouring monster-gods)!

25 golden dollars to find the Donner Party—STILL UNCLAIMED!

Another $25 to the man who can eat them alive—STILL UNCLAIMED!

$2,000 to build a working robot within a week!

$1,000 a year to foster good international relations by calling European families at random and speaking to them in English!

$5,000 to perfect your Ayn Rand impersonation!

$13,000 to start your own radio station that broadcasts nothing but sounds of airplanes landing!

$150,000 to write a book of fake trivia!

WERE YOU AWARE OF IT?

Jorge Luis Borges was the editor in chief of *Games* magazine from 1980–1981.

WERE YOU EVEN AWARE OF THIS FACT??!?

BASICS OF SNOW AND ICE WARFARE

Every youngster should, at some point, feel the bite of ice against his cheek, the feel of frost against his eye, the sensation of being buried in snow, in soundless, senseless, white eternity, for that is what death feels like. Sensitive parents who wish to protect the child from this experience do not realize that contemplation of death is a natural, healthy part of childhood. And personally, I resent their efforts to melt all the snow with giant orbiting space lenses. All this will do is encourage the children to dream instead about hot burning death from the sky. And you will agree that this is a terrible waste of giant lenses, which are desperately needed for the reading of giant books.

No. Snow and ice warfare is an inevitable ritual of childhood and may be enjoyed in many inventive variations, very few of which scar or maim. Here are some of the classic ice- and snowballs that children have always loved.

FIGURE 8: *Senate Pages Enjoying Their Once-Yearly Afternoon Off*

TABLE 7: CLASSIC ICE– AND SNOWBALLS

Name	Description
"The prize melon"	A snowball that, in weight and circumference, mimics the heft of the world's largest melon
"The come-back-here"	A snowball that is tethered to a thin leather strap or string so that it may be retrieved and used again
"The gouger"	An iceball that has been shaped by a knife and selective melting to form a sort of scythe that can easily remove an eye
"The college boy"	A regular snowball that is subsequently packed with the broken shards of a more bookish school chum's eyeglasses. This snowball should not be thrown, but forcibly fed to the bookworm for a real big laugh.
"The fine feathered friend"	A snowball with a live chickadee inserted into it. Pack tightly to prevent "beaking."
"The baked Alaska"	A snowball that has been set on fire using a common flammable gel. Less common now that child-sized asbestos gloves have been made illegal by the fainthearted.
"The Ionesco"	A snowball formed in the shape of the famous French absurdist's puffy bald head
"The truth ball"	A snowball that, when thrown properly, compels the target to tell the truth on any subject for a period of thirty to thirty-five minutes
"The squib"	A snowball that contains a small exploding capsule of fake blood (handily made at home with corn syrup, red dye, and blood). Used to frighten play-pals who may be hemophiliacs.
"The gasser"	A snowball that contains a small exploding capsule of mustard gas that will cause the other fellow to swoon. Gassers are frowned upon in most suburban areas, though they were historically common among snow warriors of the cities—especially the newsies, for whom snowballing was not just recreation, but a means of protecting valuable territory.
"The old soldier"	A snowball from 2–7 winters past, kept in a freezer or some other storage facility, and prized for its accumulation of rough freezer ice, which will scar a fellow's face. Experts estimate that within three generations this will be the only kind of snowball left. But this will change nothing: as it always has, favor in battle shall naturally flow to the fellow who has planned in advance, and especially to those whose fathers own ice factories or cryogenic head-freezing companies.

HINTS ON BUILDING SNOW FORTS

—Locate snow fort on high ground offering plenty of visibility to surrounding terrain.

—Mound a square or circular enclosure of snow walls that are wider than they are tall.

—An armory of spare snowballs may be stacked in a pyramid in the center. This pyramid is also good for the secret storage of vodka or, if defeat is certain, cyanide capsules.

—Making use of an actual, existing army fort or tower guarantees success but is considered unsporting.

—Underground tunnels should be supported by stout beams. Glass bricks are no longer fashionable.

—Watch out for wampas.

DIVERSIONS FOR THE ASTHMATIC CHILD
WHO CANNOT PLAY IN THE SNOW

But suppose you are an asthmatic child, unsuited for play in cold weather, or for labor in the chimneys, or as a sewer lackey. There are still any number of indoor amusements that will not overtax the lungs or the inhaler. For example . . .

—Inhaler whittling
—Fabrication of elaborate kites that shall never be flown
—Pill-swapping
—Bird-loathing
—Lying on the floor and staring at the ceiling
—Finding new quiet radio programs to listen to
—Hiding

WERE YOU AWARE OF IT?

While in recent years it has been beset by tragedy, NASA reminds us that there has only been one murder in the history of the space shuttle program. It occurred in 1983. While the captain, the payload specialist, the jewel thief, the mysterious art dealer, and her private secretary were all under suspicion, the first American woman in space, Sally Ride, eventually determined that only the Indian fakir had the motive, the opportunity, and the experience in confined quarters to carry out the deed.

COULD IT BE THAT THE LACK OF GRAVITY HAS SOME EFFECT ON THE BRAIN THAT ALLOWS IT TO SOLVE MYSTERIES MORE EASILY???!!!!

TOP SPOTS FOR CRABS

Reprinted from a guest column I wrote for Yes! It Is Food! *magazine, the magazine for watchers of television food programs.*

　　—At the Wisconsin Crab Hut, Chef Danny has a special that's sure to make the crab lover salivate . . . *for crabs!* He starts with only the freshest live crabs and a recipe for cooking them! He adds steam, some spices, and then plates it all with a garnish of curly parsley . . . *voilà!* The Wisconsin Crab Hut Special!

　　—At the Crab Palace in Florence, Massachusetts, Chef Tim starts with fresh-picked crab (that's crab without the shell, to you and me). He then briefly panfries it in butter, adds heavy cream, some salt, pepper, and spices, and *voilà!* You have crab . . . with a *European bistro twist!*

　　—You might be surprised to learn that The Crab Place in Columbus, Ohio, does not actually serve crabs at all! But this joint's *funky atmosphere* and *use of mallets* will sure remind you of one that does! Yup: those are real license plates and old street signs on the walls . . . right next to the old black-and-white pictures . . . of crabs!

—At the Crab Bunker in Atlanta, Georgia, you can catch your own crabs! Every night the live crabs are set loose throughout the restaurant, sometimes attacking children! (*Please:* no dogs or gulls allowed.)

—What's that, you say? A restaurant that serves only hermit crab? Well, that describes St. Paul's Crab Town *to a T!* The hermit crabs are freshly prepared using boiling water! Crush them whole at your table and find the meat using your own jeweler's glass! You don't have to be a recluse from society to enjoy them!

—Locals know the blue crabs (a kind of crab) are great at the Crab Spot in Short Hills, New Jersey. But it's the giant Alaskan crab legs that have them driving from miles around. Previously frozen, the three-foot gigantic legs are thawed, cooked with spices, doused in 151-proof rum, set on fire, and then shoved into a *four-pound individual cheesecake.*

—Sure you've heard of clams casino, but *crabs* casino? That's the name of the game at the Crab Sweat Lodge at the Arrowhead Resort and Casino on the Pequot Reservation in southern Connecticut, where the Admiral's Buffet serves—*get this*—crab *cakes!* They're available twenty-four hours a day and night, five dozen for a nickel.

—Foster's Market, in Greenfield, Massachusetts, may look like an ordinary supermarket. But work your way back through the funky, down-home aisles of food and you'll soon discover the counter manned by Chef Billy, who has something *special* up his sleeve. Chef Billy's "Seafood Salad" starts with chopped stalks of fresh celery, some lemon juice and spices, and then . . . *sea legs?!* WHAT?! I've heard of gigantic Alaskan crab legs, but what the heck are these?

"Basically, it's pollock or some other whitefish that's formed and colored and flavored to stand in when crab is not available," says Chef Billy. That's right: *imitation crab!* And here comes the secret ingredient: mayonnaise! But this isn't your average mayo! Chef Billy's comes from a plastic 10-gallon tub with a picture of an Indian on it.

Now I love mayonnaise, but I've never seen anything quite like this. "Basically, we find it's more cost-effective to buy it this way." (!)

That's it! From coast to coast, supermarkets to restaurants, old-fashioned crab shacks to European-style bistros, there's a lot to get crabby about . . . CRABS!

SECRETS OF THE MALL OF AMERICA

When I stopped being a professional literary agent, I of course had to contrive some way for me to eat and drink at the finest restaurants without paying for anything. And so I became a columnist for a national magazine of men's fitness and adventure, in which I wrote about food, drink, and cheese, which is a kind of food.

You may recall my work. My first column was on the subject of the care and feeding of great abs (excuse me: AWESOME abs). My second column was on the subject of hunting and cooking your own polar bear steaks. My third column was on the subject of the world's greatest chili recipe ever. My fourth column was also on chili. And my fifth column was on the subject of hunting and cooking your own polar bear steaks.

The problem is that there are only so many foods in the world to write about. I believe it was Julia Child who wrote in *Mastering the Art of French Cooking*, "Here are the things you can write about: abs, polar bear steaks, chili, chili, and polar bear steaks. In that order."

I did once write a column on a different subject, but my magazine never ran it. It was on ultrahot hot sauces. By this, I should say that I mean *very spicy*, and not *boiling hot*—an important distinction of the kind a professional food journalist sometimes has to make.

An example of an ultrahot hot sauce is "Dave's Insanity Sauce," which I ate on a little cracker once, and then my head hurt, and then I had to lie down. And then I was crying for a day or so.

Dave's is actually on the milder end of the ultrahot hot sauce spectrum. There is an entire category of ultrahot hot sauces that promise death. Most of them are packaged in little coffins. Some go so far as to promise not only your death, but the obliteration of the earth. I am not a person who fears death. But I could not bring myself to endorse death by ultrahotness, which is perhaps why my magazine found my piece "overly gay."

The second article of mine that was never published was about the food court at the Mall of America. I was excited to visit the nation's largest mall, but what I discovered there shocked me. It also apparently shocked my magazine, which refused to publish it on the pretense that "most of it was made up" and that "it did not involve any polar bears or polar-bear combat," which I knew was their nice way of saying "overly gay."

But you, dear reader, are seeking COMPLETE WORLD KNOWLEDGE, and so *you* shall not shy from what is revealed in this, my unexpurgated private diary of the secrets of the Mall of America.

DAY 1

At 200 million square feet, the Mall of America is the largest mall in the United States. In addition to 520 shops, two thirds of which are devoted to the sale of FDNY and NYPD baseball caps, it has a chapel and a school and a post office and an amusement park called Camp Snoopy inside of it.

It is not, I should point out, the largest mall in North America. That distinction belongs to the West Edmonton Mall, which contains 7,000 baseball-cap shops, a sausage factory, a complete medieval castle, twelve monorails, and the entire township of East Edmonton, preserved like Pompeii at the exact moment it was devoured by the West Edmonton Mall.

Still, the Mall of America is large enough that I can see it from my hotel room, literally hundreds of feet away. Its phosphor lights obliterate the Minnesota evening. It is so bright, I don't know how they get the giant bats to keep circling it.

DAY 2

The Mall of America is filled with elderly people, who are always walking, circling the mall like sharks, they say "for exercise." When they collapse, mall security discreetly removes them and props them up in the booths at Johnny Rockets.

One elderly woman has agreed to show me her favorite places to eat. Her name is Elayne. She takes me into the Odyssey Café. It is a restaurant with four dining rooms, each decorated in the style of a lost civilization. I am not very impressed by the Atlantis Room, which is just a blue room with pictures of fish on the wall. Not a single porthole, which to me just seems *obvious.*

But the Machu Picchu Room is stunning, with beautiful murals of mountaintops and very thin air, which makes it hard to breathe, and all the hard-boiled eggs are undercooked. Also, the room is staffed by actual Incas, looking sad and doing their sad little math with knots of string when not serving you omelettes. Elayne says "this is all that remains of their once-great civilization."

DAY 3

The Minnesota Picnic is a stand run by three brothers, all of them Egyptian. They serve traditional favorites of the Minnesota State Fair: pike on a stick, corn dogs on a stick, fried cheese curd, and *bamya matboukha*, the famous Egyptian okra stew, which unfortunately cannot be put on a stick.

The brothers implore me to try their new invention, deep-fried cheesecake on a stick, a stunning breakthrough in food-on-a-stick technology. Then they admit they are sad, sad like the Incas. After ten years, the mall is kicking them out and they don't know why.

I ask if maybe they are being discriminated against because they are Egyptian. Oh, no, they say. Oh. No no no no no.

DAY 4

I call the mall's PR people to ask why they are exiling the Egyptians and also to ask about the secret tunnel I found that leads from Camp

Snoopy to Pottery Barn and is lined with human skulls. This is when the Mall of America stops returning my calls. This happens sometimes when professional journalists ask the wrong questions. I'm frozen out. From here on, I'm going rogue.

DAY 5

Elayne takes me to Cereal Adventure, which is a mini theme park run by General Mills, makers of Trix and Lucky Charms and Cookie Crisp.

There is a mini golf course there, as well as an interactive exhibit on how Lucky Charms is made. Here it is shown how the leprechauns are first flayed and then pulped to be turned into the marshmallows. Off to the side are waist-high piles of abandoned little green hats that will be shipped back to Ireland under international treaty.

"Am I the only one who finds this a little bit creepy?" I ask aloud. Elayne ignores me. "You can have your picture taken and put on a box of Wheaties," she says.

That's insane, I say. I can't masturbate to a picture of myself. Where are the Mary Lou Retton boxes?

We then go to the Cereal Adventure Café, which claims to have all the General Mills cereals for sale. They have the monster cereals Boo Berry, Count Chocula, and Frankenberry. I am surprised to learn that they have never heard of Fruit Brute, which featured a werewolf. They have never heard of Yummy Mummy, who was a mummy who was fruit flavored. I wonder if they really have any business running a "cereal adventure" café at all.

DAY 6

My last interview is with a Minnesota woman who just opened a pastry shop using her grandmother's original cheesecake recipe. Her store is called Granny's Squeezecakes.

I ask her if she's tried the deep-fried cheesecake on a stick the Egyptians serve at Minnesota Picnic. She just smiles in an ominous way that makes me think she knows their days are numbered, and soon she will be cheesecake queen.

"Working in the mall is a little nerve-wracking," she confides, "because as the largest mall in the United States, we are a prime target for terrorism."

"You know what?" I say. "Fuck you."

DAY 7

My three-day journey is complete. I check in with one of the Egyptian brothers on my way out of the Mall of America.

"Did you ever discover why they are kicking us out?" he asks.

"No," I say. "The mall officials are stonewalling me. I have gone rogue," I explain.

He nods as only a sad Egyptian about to lose his deep-fry palace at the Mall of America can. "Perhaps this is for the best," he says.

He gives me something fried on a stick, and I promise to eat it someday. But for him and for me, the Minnesota Picnic is over.

PART THREE

WHAT YOU DID NOT KNOW
ABOUT THE PAST

LYCANTHROPIC TRANSFORMATION TIMETABLES

THIRD SEVENTH

	MINUTES AFTER MOONRISE/MOONSET		
	to-Wolf	to-Man	Transformation
Werewolf (North American)	9'23"	10'24"	near full, bipedal
Hombre Lobo	8'12"	8'41"	full, bidedal
Werewolf (British)	7'21"	40'23"	near full, retains language
Loup-Garou	6'28"	34'21"	general fur
Varcolac	7'12"	24'04"	pack formation
Libahunt	9'32"	35'42"	burrowing
Werebears and Skinwalkers	24'42"	29'20"	bellowing, fur

CHARM POTENCY		
silver items	medium	
wolfsbane	medium/low	
fur girdle removal	partial	
taming love of pure woman	pointless	

HISTORY'S WORST MEN'S HAIRCUTS

If all of history may be counted as a year, and human history merely the last ten seconds of that year, then you may be surprised to learn that more than two thirds of the worst haircuts in history may be contained in the slightest fraction of a millisecond in which man has played hockey. There is something about the gliding sport that attracts not only bad haircuts, but hair of the sort and texture that was once euphemistically termed by forgiving barbers as "hard-grooming": rubbery, thick, and carpetlike. As the columnist Liam Dorn wrote in the *Ontario Lamplighter* newspaper in 1928, "a hockeyist does not have hair so much as a thick, fungal covering that starts at about two inches from the circumference of his head and then grows in."

Leaving aside the Mullet, other favorites of the hockeyist included: the Scrape, the Scab, the Floppy-Dog-Ear, the Executive Floppy-Dog-Ear, and the Shag-Swoop, which was advertised as being able to somehow produce "the illusion of a mustache" and required two barbers working simultaneously and ended with the ringing of a bell.[12] Sadly, photographs do not exist, only apocryphal tales told by former hockey men who are, as you know, unreliable due to their zombie-like stupidity and puck-fever.

Yet there are many more examples outside of hockey of unusual hairstyling that have been recorded. You may ask, how is a haircut recorded for history? Obviously, sketches and photographs are invaluable. But for various reasons historians prefer those that were recorded by wax molding, a technique first employed by Charles Toobin in 1782. The Toobin Museum of Non–Hockey-Related Haircuts of Kingston, NY, is to be thanked for the following historical notes, and as well for its loving maintenance and regular dusting of thousands of categorized wax hairstyles. It is difficult, as you might guess, to keep them from melting.

---

12. For further information on such dangerous barbering practices, please see "Beard Manual," p. 91.

TABLE 8: DISCREDITED STYLES	
The Napoleon Hat 1870s–1890s, Europe and Pennsylvania	Sadly self-explanatory. Though not quite as unsightly or as difficult as its contemporary, the Tri-Corner, it was of the same period (1870s), and was much more widely practiced, being the chosen cut of the Saw Creek utopian society in the Poconos.[13] As the Creekers (as they were known) were dedicated to perfect uniformity in human shame, even the bald were asked to mimic the haircut via use of shaped hay.
The Sink Cut 1900s–1930s, North America	This quick and thrifty cut involved putting your child's head in a sink and cutting around the edge. The sink caught the blood handily. During the Depression, when many families did not have sinks, a dirt hole would be substituted, or a natural cave.
The Shot Glass 1930s, U.S. Military	An early experiment with the "Traumatic Haircut" school of American military hairstyling (along with the "High and Tight" and the "Bleeding Horseshoe") in which the dramatic shearing of the new recruit symbolically parted him from civilian life and initiated him into the regimented structure and high-paced haircut schedule of soldiering. In this case, a shot glass was placed on the new soldier's head and the rest of the hair was shaved off without lather. This generally left a single tuft of hair of varying length, which was found to be useful for tying the heads of young soldiers together for a prank (or for their own safety), but less useful in inspiring fear in the enemy. A variant, the "High and Loose," was considered by many to be exceedingly loose and quickly abandoned.

13. Please see "Utopias," p. 208.

TABLE 8: DISCREDITED STYLES *continued*

The Scamp mid-1950s, Northern U.S., Parts of Canada	The best-known exemple of the brief "moving hair" fad, in which various live animals were camouflaged and/or sewn into the hair itself, in this case, a ferret. The fad died out due to the difficulty of replacing the creatures and the high rate of hawk and eagle attacks upon citizens.
The Firefly 1970s, the cities of North America	One of several flamboyant "disco cuts," this style involved coating the tips of the hair with a common flammable gel. At a certain agreed time, the hair would be lit and used by other revelers for the purpose of freebasing cocaine. This is, of course, how Richard Pryor nearly died.
The Spitting Cobra 1970s, New York City	Via egg whites and professional styling products, the hair was shaped such that it resembled the raised hood of the snake in question. When a nearly bankrupt Manhattan was ruled by competing street gangs, each with its own signature haircut, the Spitting Cobras dominated the former fur district around Twenty-sixth Street. They were known for hissing at passersby. While the gang faded along with the forgotten Perms and Knot-tops, the haircut lived on. It was appropriated by the members of the early pre-punk band the Slithering Snakes, and then revived again by the Japanese punk revival band Wild Snake Heads. A variant, the Vader, was briefly popular among people who owned used record stores or hung out in them.

FAMOUS NOVELS THAT WERE
NOT ORIGINALLY PUBLISHED AS BOOKS

You'd be surprised to learn that many famous authors had a hard time getting published initially and had to find other outlets for their manuscripts. Other writers have simply chosen to eschew books altogether, seeking out more experimental forms. Luckily, none of the following authors chose to publish his books "electronically," for that is purely for suckers.

—*The Adventures of Tom Sawyer* by Mark Twain: originally a series of riverboat chants learned when Samuel Clemens was a pilot on the Mississippi.

—*Hopscotch* by Julio Cortazar: woven into a carpet that could be read from any direction.

FIGURE 9:

Georgian Woman Standing Upon the Novel Hopscotch

—*The Secondary Heart* by Jean-Mikhel Vizra: published as a series of sequential plaques arranged on benches in Central Park, each containing one sentence.

—*Dubliners* by James Joyce: initially telegraphed as the last message from *Titanic*. (Technically this was a series of linked short stories, the last entitled "Please Save Us from Drowning.")

—*Sessylu* by Knut Nims: actually composed of the words of *Ulysses* arranged backward. Nims never bothered to write it out this way, instead claiming that whenever *Ulysses* was read backward it was officially his work, and he deserved a royalty.

—*Seek Dark, Seek Flesh, Seek Dark Again* by Chskklkkktkkstkk: played by an autistic child on spoons.[14]

—*That Which Does Not Kill Us Is Not Good Writing*, also by Knut Nims: written into the margins of a J.Crew catalogue.[15]

---

14. Please see "Films in Which I, John Hodgman, Have Made Cameo Appearances," page 82.

15. Knut Nims is something of a cult writer whose first novel, *The Sweetest Gift of Air and Space,* was published in 1987 by Vintage to some positive critical reaction, but very poor sales.

When his publisher declined to publish his next novel, *From a Cabin in the Country*, he fired his agent, changed the name of the book *Fuck You, Too, Cowards,* and sought new representation. In his cover letter, sent to me five times in 1999, he promised "to rip the smooth white skin off American literature and expose the spreading tumor of spineless, suburban, mediocre 'fiction' that is eating the weak, atrophied muscle of art, and then to clean the wound I made with the chewing maggots of my words."

He failed to tempt anyone with this approach, and all his further works, including *Your Oh-So-Precious Properties, All the Pretty Ivy League–Type Writers Who Are Full of Shit,* and the short-story collection, *Cleveland Steamers,* were released in extremely limited editions by Nims himself, who hand-wrote each novel into the margins of J.Crew catalogues that he stole and would re-mail primarily to publishing professionals.

Yet despite this restricted audience, his iconoclasm and muscular prose attracted a devoted if small group of admirers, mainly young men. They trade his work in bootleg chapbook editions, talk about him online, and occasionally make pilgrimages to meet him at the Portland, Oregon, copy shop where he works.

"Nims rejects the priss-fiction of the writing workshop Richie Riches," writes aspiring "dirt poet" Mac Feeney on his Knut Nims fan page, "replacing all their quaint, talentless, conformist prose with hard, real words that no one writes anymore. Words like 'propinquities' and 'stentorian.'"

Though I am no longer a professional literary agent, these people still occasionally threaten my life, and Nims still sends me a novel now and again, usually on the back of a very nice Christmas card that features photos of himself and his coworkers at the copy shop that he has obviously taken without their knowledge and the typical sign-off: "Hope we can do business in the new year!"

WERE YOU AWARE OF IT?

Ruffner's *Eponyms Dictionaries Index* lists some 33,000 eponymous things or concepts, each carrying with it a name forward into history.

Many of these words[16] are named after gods or mythic figures who arguably do not require linguistic immortality, such as *cereal* or *erotica* or *juggernaut* or *Yahweh,* which I believe is a kind of British racing cap that you are never allowed to wear.

A great many more are named for medical doctors. You of course are familiar with *Bell's Palsy, Johnie McL disease, the ducts of Lushka, the columns of Morgagni, Mallory's stain, Mallory's triple stain,* and *Anton-Babinksi syndrome* (the denial of blindness with resort to confabulation by the blinded).

But were you aware that . . .

Dr. Joseph-Ignace Guillotin, inventor of the *"guillotine,"* was also its first victim?

Sixteenth-century anatomist Gabriel Fallopius, discoverer of the fallopian tube, also coined the terms palate, placenta, cochlea, and vagina—but only after his original suggestions (fallopalate, fallopenta, falloplea, and fallopagina) were rejected?

The silhouette was named for Etienne de Silhouette, the notoriously stingy finance minister to Louis XV, who ironically was himself incapable of casting a shadow, due to lycanthropy?

Continued on next page.

---

16. These Hodgman brand waders, while they are of very high quality, are not named after me.

If they were, I would have an *eponymous* relationship with them, from the Greek "named on," in which I would be the eponym. *Not* the waders. They are merely rubber pants. No one will think of me when they wear them. Unless they find the small time capsule I have hidden inside containing the text of this book, and also the small holographic message of me pleading for help, and also the poisonous viper. Then maybe they will think of me.

Tennis star Jean Rene "The Crocodile" Lacoste, who lent his name both to the Lacoste shirt and the crocodile, actually had aluminum legs?

The leotard was created by the nineteenth-century French trapeze artist Jules Leotard so that men would no longer have to "hide their best attributes"—and when not trapezing, he fought crime by night as the leotarded Parisian superhero known as the "Sad Aerialist"?

WERE YOU AWARE OF IT!?!

MORE SURPRISING EPONYMS

Hans Geigercounter
Richard J. Gatling-Gun
George Washington
  Haberdashery
Albert Shame
Sir Dennis Ballpoint
Douglasitis Brizzard
Nelly Unicyle
Alexander Graham Bell
Ampere Angstrom Alfredo
  Sauce
Paul Islets of Langerhans
Marie Eponym

FIGURE 10: *Albert Shame,*
Inventor of Same

TABLE 9: GREAT RIVALRIES IN DUNGEONS & DRAGONS

Gord 3rd-level Dwarven fighter, neutral/good	v.	Quillist 3rd-level Elven rogue, chaotic/good

Jordan Pring, Tim Randall, players

Dor Falkon 4th-level Gnomish paladin, lawful/neutral	v.	Phinax 6th-level human assassin, chaotic/neutral

Jordan Pring, Marc McDougal, players

Wistia Silverwand 2nd-level half-Elven ranger, neutral half-sister of Quillist, of royal Elven blood, in exile	v.	Devos Swifthand 3rd-level halfling thief-acrobat, chaotic/neutral

Tim Randall, Adrian Oppenheim, players

Drigael Spellweaver 9th-level Human illusionist, true neutral, DECEASED	v.	Umanzur 8th-level dark-Elven necromancer, neutral/evil

Jordan Pring, Adrian Oppenheim's fat older cousin, players

MOK 7th-level half-Orc bezerker, chaotic/evil	v.	Morquila Silverwand 9th-level Elven Psionicist, lawful/good, elfqueen and full-blooded sister of Quillist

Jordan Pring, Tim Randall, players

Dor Falkon (see above)	v.	Dor Falkon

Jordan Pring, Dungeon Master (purely a thought experiment)

A BRIEF TIME LINE OF THE LOBSTER
IN AMERICA

On a recent September afternoon, I was pleased to visit the Eastern States Exposition in Springfield, Massachusetts. "The Big E," as you perhaps know, is the great culmination of the county fair season in New England. Like many such fairs, it features the display of prize fowl and livestock, local handicrafts, ingeniously fried foods,[17] and a full, mechanized carnival featuring various rides that have been hastily assembled by angry and careless men.

It was a fine day. I saw a cow being milked by a robot. I watched recently hatched chicks in a great incubator as they lay, helpless and drenched in albumen, breathing heavily and attempting to stand. These chicks seemed to be trying to say something to me, but I could not hear them over the terrified sobbing of the children next to me. Then I went to watch the lobster judging.

It is rare that you see a real lobster competition these days. As I watched the proud young farm children in their traditional dress whites and goggles leading their well-tended lobsters about on their leashes, I wondered if these youngsters knew that, not 120 years ago, this competition would have looked very different indeed. For their enlightenment and your own, I offer this brief time line of the lobster in America.

—1890: New York socialite Frederick Geen releases 100 European lobsters in Central Park. The "great scrambling," as he called it, was part of his poetic effort to introduce to America every kind of animal ever mentioned in Shakespeare. ("[The king] forbade my tongue to speak of Mortimer. But I will find him when he lies asleep, and in his ear I'll holler 'Mortimer!' Nay, I'll have a lobster shall be taught to speak nothing but 'Mortimer,' and give it him to keep his anger still in motion." *Henry IV*) The result, however: chaos.

---

17. Please see "Secrets of the Mall of America," p. 64.

—1892: Lobsters are seen everywhere throughout New York City. They especially thrive in garbage cans, occasionally grabbing dogs and small people and pulling them in to their doom.

—1895: When a lobster kidnaps three of the four Geen Quadruplets, Frederick Geen collapses in horrid grief and never rises. His brother, the influential Horace Geen, pressures the mayor to bring in a new police commissioner to put an end to the lobster problem once and for all. Theodore Roosevelt is called in.

—1896: Discovering that the lobster cannot easily be killed except by boiling, Roosevelt instead diverts the creatures to Maine via a secret canal.

—1900–1910: Along the Maine coast, the lobster again thrives, not just on land, but for the first time in the sea. The animal previously called the "lobster" there, a kind of sea otter, faces severe competition from the new crustacean neighbors.

BERNARD LANDGRAF

FIGURE 11: *The Lobster*

—1920s: Wealthy Maine summer families regularly gather to watch the two species fight on the beach, sending servants out to egg them on with hot pokers. Pelts harvested from the "Old Lobsters" are used as very small carpets.

—1930: A law is passed that no servant shall receive more than forty new lobsters per day as food or pets.

—1932: Proving once again its old nickname, "The City That Will Not Learn from Its Errors," New York City actually imports several lobsters for display in the Central Park Zoo. The lobsters, however, rarely leave their cave, and when they do, they pace relentlessly back and forth. Zoological analysts determine that the lobsters are depressed. The lobsters are given toys to play with, small staircases to leap up, and mice to chase. Several games are developed to relieve them of their melancholy, one of which eventually becomes the board game "Monopoly." The lobsters are excellent players, and usually choose the top hat.

—1940s: Lobster-claw deformities emerge as a popular form of folk art.[18] Some Kabbalists claim that the deformed claws form the shape of secret Hebrew letters—a cryptic message from the unclean to the chosen.

—1950s: Refrigerated zeppelins make the transcontinental shipping of live lobsters a reality. Eager to be rid of them, the state of Maine pays for their tickets (coach) and creates a now-famous ad campaign to introduce the nation to the idea of eating them: "Maine Lobster: The Giant Insect That Contains Within Its Carapace the Taste of Purest Silk!"

—1968: Red Lobster opens its first restaurant in Lakeland, Florida. At the time, their famous 45 Lobster Special costs only $2.95. As a

---

18. Please see "Lobster-Claw v. Pigeon-Foot Deformities," p. 142.

publicity stunt, Frederick Geen, now 103, rises shakily from his bed for the first time in seventy-three years to personally kill the first 20,000 lobsters. He turns down the speed-boiler that Red Lobster has devised, preferring instead to strangle them one by one, weeping the entire time. The stunt is a huge success—especially among children. To this day, Red Lobster still offers diners the chance to choose their own lobster and have an old man kill it before their eyes.

—1980: The last Old Lobster finally perishes in the kitchen of the lesser-known rival chain restaurant, Furry Old Lobster. The restaurant chain then swiftly closes. It will be another decade before it is discovered that the Furry Old Lobster chain was owned by an entity called "Excellent Restaurant Concepts, Inc.," which itself is but one arm of HomarUSA. By now it will not surprise you to learn that HomarUSA is the largest lobster-owned company in the nation.

It is a sad story, true, but no sadder than much of history. And perhaps it will cheer you to know that the Blue Ribbon at the Big E went to young Amanda Dearborn and her handsome young crustacean, Brock.

FILMS IN WHICH I, JOHN HODGMAN, HAVE MADE CAMEO APPEARANCES

Occasionally, films and television series require a tweedy literary personality who is asthmatic and has a somewhat lazy eye. It is a cliché, of course, but one I am not ashamed to embody. So from time to time Hollywood calls my observatory, usually after they have called George Plimpton and have learned that he passed away in 2003.

I have appeared in a number of movies, often in very minor roles; but I think my films nonetheless tell an interesting story of the American cinema, at least from the lazy-eyed point of view.

—*Mimic*: In this horror film, giant bugs come to me for literary advice. I explain to them that I am no longer a professional literary agent. "I am out of the advice business," I say. They leave in disgust. Cockroaches, after all, do not retire; they endure.

Later the cockroaches return with an autistic child who understands their strange click language. Via clicking, they ask again for my help with their novel. I explain that unless they have a *written* language, they are out of luck. "With rare exceptions,"[19] I tell them, "publishers are not in the market of publishing novels that are not written down and instead are performed by live autistic children clicking spoons together. The shipping costs are simply prohibitive."

Then the bugs kill me. Fun fact from the set: I do not remember the name of the young actor who played the autistic child. But I do remember that between takes he was either *very* high, or *very* autistic. Anyway, we partied.

—*The Muppet Movie*: This was a movie about puppets who go to Hollywood to become stars. As they travel, they frequently consult the script of the movie in order to know what to do next. When they reach Hollywood, they begin making a movie about the movie the viewer has just been watching. The puppets build plywood simulacra of props that, earlier in the film, were presented as real. Then the roof of the soundstage smashes in and a powerful rainbow shines down and obliterates everything, including a plywood imitation of the fake rainbow that had appeared in the first scene. The frog and bear and pig simulations panic as the fake/real and real/fake worlds nearly destroy each other. The puppets then look directly into the camera and instruct the viewer that "life's like a movie: write your own ending."

This was the only film in which the French literary critic Roland Barthes received a screenplay credit (he also did uncredited work on *Corvette Summer*). I appeared in it as a favor to him, playing "The

---

19. See "Famous Novels That Were Not Originally Published as Books," p. 74.

Tweed-Wearing Bearded Man" who keeps yelling "The author is dead!" from the end of the sleazy bar in which the frog puppet meets the bear puppet. I recall getting either high or autistic on the set with the film's composer, Paul Williams. Elliott Gould may have been there too. "Paul," I said, "or Elliott: This whole thing is exceedingly effed-up. I can't even *grow* a beard."

—*Just Cause*: I appear in a short scene at the beginning of this largely forgotten film as a lazy-eyed law professor opposite Sean Connery. Sean Connery *could* grow a beard, let me tell you. And he often did so, on command, just for laughs. However, for my scene with him, in which we debate the death penalty, Connery was replaced by a sophisticated puppet.

—*Crimson Tide*: This is a movie about Denzel Washington and Gene Hackman fighting on a submarine. I played the professorial, tweed jumpsuit–wearing Ship's Creative Writing Counselor (or "Counsie" in submarine slang[20]). Most of my part was cut out, but I did get to sing a sea shanty, a longtime dream, before my character was then killed by Gene Hackman's fist.

—*Gimme a Break!* (TV, several episodes): Producer Alan Landsburg, whom I had known from consulting on the Honey Island Swamp Monster episode of his *In Search of . . .* series, asked me to step in as the "father figure" in this situation comedy after the untimely death of actor Dolph Sweet, "the Chief." For several episodes I played Phineas, a friendly, eccentric, and extremely bookish alien who had been charged by my planet to observe Nell Carter and the three girls she cared for.

After Sweet's passing, my character emerged from the attic crawl space where I had been spying on them and explained that their love for one another in this time of crisis, which I had witnessed through

---

20. Please see "Short Words For Use on Submarines to Preserve Oxygen," p. 133.

my intricate array of hidden peepholes, had at last inspired me to re-tract my alien antennae for good and try to become human.

I also proclaimed my passion for the character of Nell, and frequently tried to impress her with my strange powers (stopping time, levitating, draining fish tanks with a vacuum cleaner). She would hide her obvious affection for me with boisterous abuse ("You interplanetary numbskull!" she would often shriek, to my delight), while seeking to hide the truth of my nature from the bumbling NASA investigator played by a young Jonathan Silverman. Gradually it became clear that Nell, despite her salty retorts, was falling in love with me.

I am sad to report that the producers quickly shut down this provocative storyline and brought in Joey Lawrence to replace me in a non-alien role. They said it was not a matter of my being white and Nell black—that could be explained away by the fact that I was an alien, and on my planet the whites *were* the blacks. The problem was, they said, that I was *excessively tweedy*. America was not ready, they said, to accept a relationship between a working-class woman and an obviously wealthy, literary dilettante who also happened to be an alien. It is a shame. Say what they will, she was the most giving lover I've ever had.

PROHIBITION-ERA EUPHEMISMS FOR ALCOHOL

The noble experiment of 1920–1933 didn't stop anyone from drinking, of course. But the dubious quality of bootleg liquor and homemade toadstool hooch[21] did cause sufficient brain damage among the speakeasy set such that simple, useful descriptors were maniacally replaced with the zippy, jazz-age lingo of the insane. Broadway was "That Great Glowing Gulch of Drowning Dreams," tough guys were "gorillas," and gorillas were "mega-chimps." But by far the

---

21. Please see p. 87 regarding this phenomenon.

greatest number of euphemisms was reserved for booze itself, that "numbing nectar of the forbidden fruit of the old alcohol tree!" Here are some of the more famous . . .

Devil's tears

Sleepy syrup

Zip sauce

Hop tallow

Trance juice

Grain guzzle

Massage oil

Mystery nip

Irish vinegar

French mayonnaise

Brain shellac

Distillate of dreamtime

Jazz chowder

Fairy pee

Corn cologne

Washcloth wringings

Genuine gin-flavored beverage

The sweet tonic of olde

That slippery serum

Romulan ale

Near beer

Stutter milk

Juniper jizz

Antimatter

Stun gravy

WERE YOU AWARE OF IT?

The famous Cole Porter tune "I'm In, You're In" was actually Porter's typically wry response to the urine-drinking craze of the 1920s.

The practice originated with the fierce reindeer herders of Siberia known as the Koryac, who centuries ago had devised a means of purifying the hallucinogenic toadstool known as *fly agaric.* A local shaman would eat the mushroom, using his body to filter out the poisonous muscarine; its mood-altering compounds were preserved in his urine, which was then ritually consumed by other Koryac and also some of the more favored reindeer.

Marco Pensworthy, a monocled young libertine and staff member of the American Museum of Natural History, who was later dismissed for seducing the skeleton of a giant ground sloth, introduced the custom to New York. During prohibition, many a tuxedoed, thrill-thirsty swell attended one of Dr. Marco's private "Siberian Tea Parties," beneath the frozen gaze of the stampeding elephants of the Hall of African Mammals, where, wrote Porter . . .

> *There isn't any shame in*
> *Meeting with the Shaman*
> *And making like the reindeers do . . .*
> *It's just a little wonder*
> *That will unfreeze your tundra*
> *I'm in, you're in. You're in, too.*

After his disgrace, Pensworthy would wander Central Park humming Porter's tune and offering passersby swigs from a suspicious flask. Finally arrested and institutionalized, he trepanned himself to death in 1952.

DOG PEOPLE V. CAT PEOPLE

TABLE 10: HISTORICAL DOG FANCIERS	
General Howe, Commander of the British Forces during the American Revolution	His Irish Wolfhound, "Sardine," sometimes joined him for dinner.[22]
Victoria Woodhull, free-love advocate, first woman candidate for president (1872)	Shared rooms with "Sprinks," a Norwegian Elkhound. In the nineteenth century, this provocative arrangement was known as a "Boston Marriage."
Eugene V. Debs, socialist	Wrote long letters from his prison cell to his Hungarian Vizsla, "Szandor."
Linus Pauling, Nobel Prize–winning chemist	Fed massive doses of vitamin C to his Schipperke, "Josef."
Jack Lemmon, actor	Took delight in tossing raw steaks to his Brazilian mastiff, "Diego," and also to Walter Matthau.
Truman Capote, author of *In Cold Blood*	Hosted his famous "Black and White Ball" while riding atop his monstrous Newfoundland, "Manfredda."
Marlon Brando, actor	Fed his Oscars to his Catahoula Leopard Dog, "Mai-Mai."

22. Sardine was adept at carving at the table, and Howe trusted all his roasts and joints to this ungainly wiry-coated companion. Yet because Sardine was trained in England, he could never master the carving of the wild turkeys native to the colonies, inspiring Benjamin Franklin to nominate the turkey as the national bird (please see "Colonial Jobs Involving Eels," p. 203). When Sardine's master was defeated, Sardine immediately went blind and never spoke again. He eventually died at sea while returning to England.

DOG PEOPLE V. CAT PEOPLE
CONTINUED

TABLE 11: THEIR CORRESPONDING NUMBER ON THE CAT SIDE		
Daniel Boone	Doted on his American Curl, "Lila," even when devising forty-six ways of skinning cats (many still used today).	 **FIGURE 12:** *Daniel Boone in Coat of Cat-Fur Trim*
Rasputin, Russian mystic and occultist	Made a bed for his Russian Blue, "Tania," out of locks of virgins' hair and snakes.	
Gerald Ford, former football player, president	Often walked around the White House with his obese Manx, "Leslie," draped across his shoulders.	
Rosey Grier, former football player, needlepoint expert	Would frequently sing "It's All Right to Cry" to his British Shorthair, "Daniel."	
Billy Ocean, singer	Briefly had his own televised variety show with his Cornish Rex, "Meow-Meow," called *Billy Ocean and Meow-Meow*.	

SOME WHO OWNED FOUR
OR MORE DOGS . . .

This list does not include owners of hunting dogs—only those who owned multiple dogs as a hobby. While keeping and training packs of dogs to hunt may be bloodthirsty, it does not mean that you are insane or enjoy smelling bad.

Ingrid Bergman
Sammy Davis, Jr.
Vladimir Horowitz
Benny Hill
Madeleine Albright
Baby Spice

SOME WHO OWNED FIFTEEN
OR MORE CATS . . .

In this case, I include those cats that were kept for hunting.

Legs Diamond
Ron Wood
Martin Scorsese
Orville Redenbacher
Howard Dean

ONE WHO OWNED
THOUSANDS AND THOUSANDS
OF CRICKETS . . .

Alexander Graham Bell

WERE YOU AWARE OF IT?

Jack Ruby owned seventeen dachshunds, whom he referred to as "his children." In an astonishing coincidence, all of his dogs were named either Lincoln, Kennedy, or Oswald, except one, which was named "Li'l Grassy Knoll."

Meanwhile, Jaqueline Kennedy kept seventeen *cats*. She disliked the animals, but kept a pack of trained felines for the hunting of voles. This was an ancient European pastime akin to fox hunting, but replacing the dogs with cats, the fox with voles and/or shrews (moles and mice are disqualifiers), and the horses with single-speed bicycles. Her passion for the sport, which bordered on addiction, was considered a potential liability by some within the White House, who feared that many in mainstream America, who rarely eat vole, would perceive the sport as an aristocratic European fancy. Still, it was practiced on the sly, and as a result, most of Washington, D.C., is still voleless.

BEARD MANUAL

Due to lack of popularity and high insurance premiums, most styling manuals no longer even mention these challenging beards, chops, and mustaches. The following guide first appeared in 1948's *The Potts Barber Colleges' Bloodless Guide to Beards and Burnsides*, later reissued in 1970 as *A Barber Prepares*. While bootleg instructions for these styles still circulate on the Web, they require considerable experience and specialized equipment and are best left to expert barbers only.

TABLE 12: FOR EXPERT BARBERS ONLY		
Name	Needed Equipment	Rate of Difficulty
Starchops	Junk shears, true shears, rag shears, badger brush, razor	97.9
The Continental Merlin	Electric razor with No. 5 and No. 9 attachments, mounted serially	92.7
Hashburns	Double shears, straight razor, mezzaluna razor, blood-sop, pestle	90

FIGURE 13:
Another Stumper

The Van Catfish	Straight razor, whiskering iron, style pliers, catfish	89.3
The Startled Satan	Feather razor, kerosene, hair-blighter, curling clasps, strong leather straps or other restraints	87.5
The Flaxen Neck	Texturing shears, thumbnail shears, hard wire comb, medium wire comb, scraper, feathering paste, plenty of cotton, beer	86.2

SOME PROPHETS WHO WERE
NOT ACTUARIES

—ASKOLD THE VIKING, goes the legend, predicted the discovery of North America and psychically guided Leif Eriksson to the site of his first settlement in Newfoundland.

Askold was an unusual Viking in that he did not advise pillage and decimation via flying longboat, but peaceful coexistence with the new continent's indigenous peoples. And so he did not predict the resistance of Nonosabasut, wizard-chief of the Beothuks of Newfoundland.

Nonosabasut, historians now believe, was the first to suggest that the Vikings wore horned helmets, which really annoyed the Vikings and was never true. Then he conjured a horrible blizzard: a mini ice age that would drive the Vikings back, not only out of Canada but from their strongholds in Greenland as well. Finally Nonosabasut's icy anger reached further: to Askold himself. Despite the Viking's psychic pleas for mercy, the spell finally touched his heart and instantly froze it solid.

Nonosabasut had repelled the invaders, but the effort tired him. He lived for only 700 years more—400 fewer than was expected of his line—and his exhaustion left his land unguarded against the French and the British. Their settlements would eventually drive the Beothuk into the interior, where Nonosabasut's people scraped a meager existence from the mud and dwindled.

Nonosabasut's descendant, Shanawdithit, was the last of the known Beothuk. She came to live with the English in St. John's, Newfoundland, and is the source for most of what we know about Beothuk culture. There she would tell of Nonosabasut's regret that he had wasted his energy in repelling the Vikings, insofar as their culture and infectious diseases were comparatively much easier on the Beothuk than those of the Europeans, who actually did wear horned helmets. Shanawdithit and her culture finally died together of tuberculosis in 1829. She had been rechristened Nancy.

—*BINONAI CULL*, the "Seer of Saratoga," owned a popular nail and tack store before his wife was trampled by a horse in 1940. Crippled with grief, he fell into a sleeping trance that lasted for the rest of his life. He never spoke in full voice again, but once an hour he would mumble in a whisper. At his bedside, his sister-in-law, Marie Chester, scribbled down what she had heard. They were startling predictions—that soon "computing machines" would be common; that by the century's end the nation would be linked by great high-speed roads of smooth macadam; and that scientists would finally learn how to induce mustache growth in children.

While Cull's visions were initially dismissed as fantasy, his correct prediction of the attack on Pearl Harbor garnered Cull and Chester international fame. Pilgrims came to his bedroom from around the country to seek his inaudible counsel—some of them, it is rumored, emissaries from the War Department seeking strategic advice.

After the war, a world tour was quickly scheduled and a rolling bed swiftly designed. Cull and Chester visited Rome, London, and Paris, where they wed in 1947. The marriage of Chester to a sleeping man raised some eyebrows, but not as many as his early television program on the DuMont Network, *The Cull and Chester Trance Afternoon* (1948).

Though a daily three-hour-long program featuring nothing but a static shot of an unconscious tuxedoed man mumbling to the camera would probably not succeed today, early adopters of television were rapt. Perhaps overly so. After three months, hundreds of viewers wrote in complaining of nausea or unexplainable levitation while watching, and some three dozen seem to have become completely hypnotized. Across DuMont's three markets—New York, Pittsburgh, and Washington, D.C.—these viewers sleepwalked into their kitchen, where they baked menacing black cakes that no one dared to eat. Three of the cakes are kept in the Museum of Television and Radio in New York, and one was thoroughly studied by scientists. The ingredients are still undetermined.

The resulting bad publicity contributed to the demise of the

DuMont Network, and the television industry was forced to adopt its first Anti–hypnosis Pledge. Cull, for his part, died in 1958 and ceased making predictions in 1964. His last words to his grieving widow: "Thank you for all you have done. You will join me, darling, when come the mustachioed children." She still lives today.

—*SARAH WOODHOPE* grew up in the suburbs around Boston and was noted in her high school yearbook as the school's only zither player and its first practicing Wiccan. In the fall of 1985, at the age of seventeen, she had a strange and vivid dream: a Patriot win over the heavily favored Dolphins in the AFC championship. She only mentioned the dream to one or two friends. But when it came true, she tearfully confessed that she had been dreaming of sporting events every night since she had gotten into Bryn Mawr early. She saw flashes of hockey games, whole innings of baseball that would not be played until the following summer, the tips of Larry Bird's fingers releasing the ball in what would be the last NBA game he would ever play. "I never asked for this," she told the *Boston Globe* when her strange gift became known. "Why would Gaia put these awful images in my head? I only wish it would stop."

Woodhope's visions continued, however, and Bostonians will recall that she eventually agreed to share them once a week with local disc jockey Dale Dorman during his drivetime shift on KISS-108. Her glimpses of the sporting future did not always predict a winner, and indeed they were often incomplete and imperfectly understood by Woodhope herself: She never quite grasped the rules of football, for example, and expressed surprise when she was told that William "The Refrigerator" Perry was an actual human and not a fantastic invention of her unconscious. "I thought . . . ," she said in a laughing declaration that would be played by Dorman again and again over the years, "I thought he was some kind of beautiful ogre!" At the end of each segment, Woodhope would explain a principle of Wicca and encourage the listeners to help heal the earth through enlightened white magick. This was her condition for appearing, and her advocacy is at least partly responsible for the large number of covens in Boston today, as well as the tradition of burning incense before Bruins games.

The following September, Woodhope went to Bryn Mawr, where she became an English major and would go on to write feminist fantasy novels. According to her autobiography, *Cauldron Sister*, her dreams ceased once she left Massachusetts, much to her relief. But there was one final vision she held back from Dorman: She dreamed of a short grounder along the first-base line, the ball hop-rolling gaily through the legs of an instantly ruined Bill Buckner and continuing on over the queasy green outfield at Shea Stadium. It was, of course, Game 6 of the upcoming 1986 World Series. This was the first time, she wrote, that she actually understood what she had seen, and what it would mean to Dorman and his listeners: that Boston would have to wait another eighteen years before it could break the curse laid on the Red Sox by Babe Ruth, that noted warlock of swat.

"I couldn't put that kind of sadness out into the world," she wrote, "especially since I knew it would only come back to me threefold: that is the Law." Still, an unlikely friendship had developed between the DJ and the composed young witch, and so on her last broadcast that Labor Day, she kept her silence, offering only a hopeful Wiccan farewell: *"Hoof and horn, hoof and horn, all that dies shall be reborn. Corn and grain, corn and grain, all that falls shall rise again. So mote it be!"*

PART FOUR

WHAT YOU DID NOT KNOW ABOUT HOBOES

LYCANTHROPIC TRANSFORMATION TIMETABLES

FOURTH SEVENTH

	MINUTES AFTER MOONRISE/MOONSET		
	to-Wolf	to-Man	Transformation
Werewolf (North American)	8'43"	15'00"	full, with pants
Hombre Lobo	7'10"	10'12"	full, naked, savage
Werewolf (British)	6'24"	45'34"	full, bipedal
Loup–Garou	5'22"	49'32"	full, pure wolf
Varcolac	6'53"	29'43"	full quadripedal
Libahunt	7'23"	38'23"	full, monstrous
Werebears and Skinwalkers	19'09"	30'42"	rampage

CHARM POTENCY

silver items	only bullets
wolfsbane	low
fur girdle removal	impossible
taming love of pure woman	woman is eaten

ACTIVE

HOBO MATTERS

They called it the War to End All Wars. They called it the London Fire and the Trail of Tears. But they were all wrong. It was called the Great Depression, and the hoboes saw it coming.

1929, October. Black Thursday. The 24th day of October, 1929: the day the stock market crashed, instantly wiping out $30 billion in stock value. Soon after, the Bank of the United States would collapse, trapping all inside, many of them orphans. From his hoveryacht in the Caspian Sea, President Hoover reassured the panicked nation that only foreigners and the mentally feeble would suffer. But the damage was too great. After a decade of high-flying prosperity, the United States' economy fell to earth and began tunneling to an awful volcanic core of despair, food riots, cloying folk songs, and lava. By March, 250,000 apple sellers would crowd the streets of Manhattan, desperately refusing to sell any other kind of fruit. But apples and sellers alike were easy picking . . . for the hoboes.

There had been hoboes in the United States since there had been trains and liquor, which is to say: always. But by 1930, an estimated two million broken souls had taken to the wandering life, hopping boxcars, picking up work where they could find it, and drinking, drinking, drinking. When prohibition reigned, the hoboes knew of secret stills and hidden lakes of moonshine. It made them strong and willful, and it made them blind and disfigured, and it spurred them to sing strange guttural songs in croaking voices that haunted the American night.

In many ways, they were a nation unto themselves. They had their own currency in the form of "hobo nickels"—the ordinary buffalo nickels onto which they would intricately carve new words and images, changing the Indian head to a picture of a hobo or changing the buffalo into a large hairy man wearing a cloak and fake horns. Another common craft was lint-knitting, using scraps of wool fuzz from pilled sweaters to make new sweaters, which they would then attempt to sell door to door. They had their own flag, which was identical to the flag of Barbados (this was either a coincidence or a deliberate effort to confuse).

FIGURE 14: *"The Hobo Standard"*

And they devised a secret language of signs and scrawls used to alert their passing brethren to danger or opportunity. A crucifix chalked on the side of a house meant that religious talk would get you a free meal inside. A picture of a cat meant "a kind woman lives here." But intersecting circles warned that the local sheriff carried throwing stars, while twin Ws meant a mean dog slept in the yard and would rise on two legs and whisper secrets if you slept in the bushes. On some alley walls in whistle-stop towns you might find a cryptic translation of the complete text of *Tristram Shandy*, as that was the hobo's favorite novel. And a picture of an H with sunrays around it meant that the hour had come: it was time to overthrow the government of the United States.[23]

When in the spring of 1932 great masses of unemployed veterans descended upon Washington to urge the passing of the Bonus Bill, hoboes came with them. Under the leadership of Joey Stink-Eye Smiles, they infiltrated the White House, pocketing sandwiches and

---

23. See "Some Useful Hobo Signs," p. 117.

replacing Secretary of the Treasury Ogden Mills with one of their own, Hobo Joe Junkpan. And across the country they began a coordinated reign of terror: soiling featherbeds, salting the cornfields, and dancing manic, heavy-footed jigs on parlor floors while ordinary citizens looked on in horror. In Kansas City, a hobo declared himself Duke of All the West and began demanding tithes. They wanted cheap beer and warm hats. They wanted bent nails and pieces of string. They demanded half barrels of swallowfeather sauce, and no one knew what they were talking about.

FIGURE 15: *Secretary of the Treasury Hobo Joe Junkpan*

At his inauguration in 1933, a new crippled president named Roosevelt addressed the nervous crowd: "The people of the United States have not failed. In their need, they have registered a mandate that they want direct, vigorous action. And so I will kill all the hoboes, and together we will gnaw on their bones." It was time for a comprehensive Hobo Eradication Plan called "The New Deal."

The president acted swiftly. He established the Civilian Conservation and Hobo Fighting Corps. He took the country off the gold standard, denying the hoboes the use of their precious teeth. The Works Progress Administration was created largely as a cover for Walker Evans, photographer by day, hobo hunter by night. He had only one target: Joey Stink-Eye Smiles. But Smiles was slippery, twice eluding the photographer's poisoned darts before disappearing into a ditch or a shrub. Now it was war. The hoboes retaliated by sneaking up behind the White House and whistling very loudly. They wrote confusing, illiterate editorials. And they summoned giant dust storms that stalked the land, eroding topsoil and swallowing small towns whole.

Finally the president knew there was only one way to end the hoboes' march across the blighted land: polio. Alone in his secret White House lab, Roosevelt created a concentrated serum of the dreaded disease that would be placed in the nation's water supply by the Tennessee Valley Authority. According to his contemporaries, Roosevelt was tortured by this decision. He knew that a certain number of non-hobo citizens would spend the rest of their lives in iron lungs as a result of his actions, but it would finally put a stop to the wandering people—starting at their feet and ending at their waists.

But then came Pearl Harbor. Some say Roosevelt knew the Japanese would attack that infamous December 7th. The truth is, he didn't. But the hoboes did. And as the tragic war that followed put a final end to the Great Depression, so too did it put an end to the hobo war. As quickly as they had come, the hoboes mysteriously disappeared. No one knows where they went, or why. Some say they found patriotism in their hearts, joining the war against a common enemy. Others say they went to the stars or to another dimension. And still others say they live on today, moving quietly from town to town, preparing for the time when their great chicken-bone and moonshine empire will rise again. Is it possible? No, because historians agree that they almost certainly went to the stars.

But if you live near a railway track and listen as the train passes, it is almost as if you can still hear them singing—the dark and lonely wind of history still blowing from their rotted lungs.

BRIEF LIVES OF SOME NOTABLE HOBOES

QUEEN MYRA NELSON, THE LADY STRANGE

Every August the hoboes would cease their lonely wandering to attend the National Hobo Convention in Britt, Iowa,[24] to trade tales and trousers and to elect a hobo queen. But it is hard to tell how many hoboes were actually women, as even many of the men wore fake beards. Hoboes certainly did not marry, preferring solitude, alcohol, cold sunrises, coarse lint, and crisp chicken skin (in that order) to love.

This was true enough of the best-known hobo queen, Myra "Strangey" Nelson, who became famous in the non-hobo world as the reticent object of H. L. Mencken's affection. Mencken had met her in 1909 while writing about a Baltimore soup-and-whiskey kitchen for *The Sun*. Nelson was wide-shouldered and strong, with sleepy gray eyes that Mencken wrote "stripped my soul acid-like of the corrosion of cynicism. She made me an odd believer in those novelistic passions I still despise, yet cannot deny."

They got to talking, and he wooed her with sly talk of Boobus Americanus and Darwin. "Obviously we are apes," she replied. "Look at my teeth, silly man!"

Mencken secretly went to her coronation in Britt in 1910, but when he revealed that he had followed her there, she attempted to stab him with a knife. He continued to chase her periodically over the next five years, but she consistently refused him. Embittered, Mencken wrote a biting essay entitled "The Lady Strange: The Woman Incapable of Love," which remains the source of many of our myths about hobo women: that they do not understand the word "kiss"; that their ruthless manliness misshapes their brains and makes them fear affection; that they raise cougars as pets and eat them; that they have incredibly veiny arms.

---

24. Please see "The States, Their Nicknames and Mottoes, and Other Facts Critical to Safe Travel," p. 158.

None of this is true, of course, and Queen Myra, whose arms were beautiful and whose cougar lived long, reportedly laughed it off. Mencken, however, regretted his anger for the rest of his life: His 1918 "In Defence of Women" is considered by many scholars to be his apology to his hobo love.

MINDBENDER STEVE

The hoboes did not leave many records. Those who were not illiterate were intensely superstitious and especially distrustful of ink. Unlike chalk, it could not be washed away by rain and time, and thus was considered by the hobo to be a perversion. Hoboes considered forgetting to be an honor to the world, which of course forgot each moment as it passed. And in the makeshift railyard camps called "jungles," it was considered a virtue if you could legitimately and purposefully forget anything that had happened to you a week, a day, an hour before. It was for this reason that, while they loathed books, they loved magazines, and indeed would often congregate in periodical rooms of local public libraries to commune with the old news, the fleeting and forgotten, and also to sleep and fart.

The exception was Mindbender Steve, the hobo poet, who scratched out tales of boxcar life in the margins of the newspapers he had fashioned into undergarments. Several of them were published in 1916 in *The Appeal to Reason*, a socialist newspaper out of Girard, Kansas, that regularly romanticized the hobo life. As evidenced in his "Hobo's Code," Mindbender's poems offered a rare glimpse into the life and philosophy of hoboism, and they always, always rhymed:

> *A hobo always goes and goes*
> *He does not stop to change his clothes*
> *He rides the rails that he has chose.*
> *Water pours out from a hose!*
>
> *Do not show me tramp or bum*
> *Tramp may ride, and bum's a chum*

But both beg from the other one.
Kids: stop chewing chewing gum!

Neither works like hobo does
Carving coin and twisting fuzz
Into a pretty pair of gloves.
The past tense of "to be" is "was"!

A hobo he will never steal
Unless it is to get a meal
Or cash, or gems, or fur of seal.
Some Japanese eat broiled eel!

But saddest: those who do not ride
At all, but stand and die inside
As world spins on and throws aside
The past, and hope, and faith, and pride.
In one direction do trains glide
Not looking back, on windward side,
Across the continent's divide
The hobo rides and rides and rides.
I will eat anything that's fried!

The hoboes, themselves, however, hated Mindbender for committing their culture to paper, and the *Appeal* received several angry letters, all of them written in chalk or spit, many of them on fire. Mindbender died in a Paris hotel in 1937. His last published work, a letter to the *New Yorker*: "Many still feel I have committed some sin by creating hobo poetry. All I can say is: at least it is not cowboy poetry."

KARL MALDEN

Young Malden Sekulovich, of Gary, Indiana, was an itinerant steelworker and boxcar poet for years before becoming a famous film and television star. As a hobo, he took the name "Kaveman

Karl" and was known for hosting hobo stomp dances on his enormous nose. He was drawn to the stage in the late thirties, when hoboes were enjoying something of a vogue on Broadway, starring in such hobo-themed shows as *Railbirds!* and *A Streetcar Named Desire.* Later in his career, he became the American Express spokesperson, immortalizing the line "Never leave home without it, especially if you plan to forever lead a nomad's life on the hard hobo road, dodging the bulls and sleeping in makeshift hobo jungles and eating only beans, paste, and freedom."

Michael Douglas, his young costar in *The Streets of San Francisco*, recalled once that Malden would often take him aside and encourage a life of hoboism on the young star.

As Douglas told *Rolling Stone* in 1979: "Malden would say, 'Come on, brother! Let's leave all of this star stuff behind and go a-roamin'!' But that was never my trip, and he knew it. And then Karl would gaze out the window, with this sad look on his face. I used to think he was just staring stupidly the way old people do sometimes. Now I think probably he was looking at the scenery, angry that it wasn't moving."

HOBO JOE JUNKPAN

A trusted friend of King Joey Stink-Eye Smiles, Junkpan was the only hobo to serve as Secretary of the Treasury of the United States. While he held office for only seventeen days, he managed to institute a few policies still on the books today: the repeal of the overcoat tax, for example, as well as the creation of the alternative minimum tax; his hobo signature, a picture of a dog wearing a hat, is still found on certain collectible runs of dollar bills. A quiet, hollow-cheeked man, he by all accounts took his brief tenure very seriously. While his hobo protectors held jamborees in his office (which are said to have attracted some of the younger members of the Treasury staff), Junkpan kept to himself, nude, meticulously chalking pinstripes onto his only suit of clothes by the light of a pile of burning bonds. Only when this task was complete did he announce his most sweep-

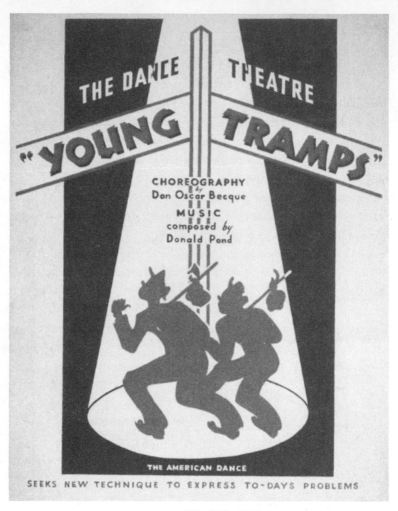

FIGURE 16: *The Hobo Vogue*

ing reform: "From here on, everyone will be allowed to supplement their income by making their own nickels—hobo-style—out of existing nickels, or lint, or any metal they might find. These shall be legal tender. Pennies and such will still be minted by pros. But nickels are fair game for all Americans." Those who heard these words over the sound of the banjo and hobo chanting dismissed it as nonsense, and Junkpan and his ilk were soon scoured from the Treasury by Hoover's pneumatic militia.[25] But most economists agree that the Nickels Are Fair Game Plan would have swiftly solved the Great Depression, and in fact is used today in India, where the sallow face of Junkpan still stares out from many homemade five-rupee pieces.

---

25. Hoover's cadre of fighting, pneumatic robots was but one of the amazing technological advances he obtained from the visionary inventor Nikola Tesla. By the 1930s, Tesla lived in near poverty, having endured a mottled career of success and heartbreaking failure. He never gained patent or credit for his discovery of the radio or X-rays; and his long

battle with his former mentor, Edison, over which was the best electric current—Tesla's alternating current or Edison's direct—had culminated in a giant lightning fight that had left him scarred both physically and emotionally. Hoover might have revived Tesla's reputation. But he saw a colder (though admittedly more cost-effective) path in stealing ideas directly from Tesla's dreams. As Tesla slept, Hoover sent agents into his room at the Waldorf-Astoria equipped with one of Tesla's own Dream-Coils, and thus gained the secrets to the Long Range Death Ray, the Mechanical Snake, the Ultra-Car, the Hover-Yacht, and many more revolutionary devices. Hoover was glad of them when the hoboes attacked. But in the very twilight of his presidency, wary of how history would judge a dream-thief, he ordered all of the prototypes and their designs destroyed. They are now gone forever.

FIGURE 17: *Herbert Hoover with Dream-Thieving Machine*

BOGMAN ZEKE

Not actually a hobo, but a leathery, preserved two-thousand-year-old corpse that was carried around by the hobo Electric Elbow Donny (an "electric elbow" was a hobo known for wearing small razors on his elbows for carving out sleeping space on a crowded boxcar floor, as opposed to a "three elbow," who was a deformed person). It is unclear how Donny came into possession of Zeke, but they never parted, and Donny credited the Bogman for helping him give up booze, although Donny often said this while drunk. Zeke was by all accounts a handsome corpse, though his face was moldy and had been somewhat flattened by the centuries he spent in the peat bog that prevented his complete decay. Most agree he was probably the victim of a ritual murder by ancient druids, who hated hoboes.

JOEY STINK-EYE SMILES

The most famous hobo king, Joey Stink-Eye Smiles, was born Gordon P. Wister, Jr., on Washington's Birthday, 1910, to an attorney and his wife in Bronxville, New York.

On the child's third birthday, Gordon P. Wister, Sr., discovered three hoboes on his porch in the still blue light of morning. With a friendliness he would come to regret, he gave them ham and fresh milk.

The hoboes thanked him and explained that they were looking for the reincarnation of their dead hobo king, Grand Head Pipe Charles Noe. The hoboes' blind dog, Punch, was a kingsniffer, they said, one of dozens of dogs the hoboes bred to track down the new king, and so Punch had led them to this town.

"But you have no dog," noted Gordon senior.

The three hoboes looked back and forth at one another sheepishly. Punch had left them there to check out another house, they said. And now they were cold—could they come in and warm their filthy feet by the fire? The whole story seemed suspicious. But again taking pity, Gordon senior admitted them. That is when they first saw Gordon junior sitting upon the stair, fashioning with little hands a miniature bindle stick and wearing a full beard. The hoboes immediately knelt before him.

As Gordon junior's father and now his mother, Molly, watched, uncomprehending, the hoboes arrayed upon the stair a selection of junk and bric-a-brac from a burlap bag. The child instinctively identified the three items that had belonged to the dead king: a snuff box full of dead flies, a chain of paper clips, and an unfinished pork chop. The hoboes wrote upon the wall in coal, and the child quickly deciphered the code, speaking aloud the old hobo saying: "Hobo Queens Are Crowned, but Hobo Kings Are Found." And so he was.

The hoboes explained that they wished to take the child to Britt and make him their king. He would be happy, cared for, and beloved, they assured his parents. He would never have to bathe, they promised, and they could still see their son, from time to time, if they went to the train-yard and kept their distance. In addition to all this, they said, they could also offer the family a very fine lint scarf.

Gordon senior stuttered a dry protest: he was an American and a realist and meritocrat—he would not see his son taken to take part in some backward railyard royalty. But Molly Wister saw plainly the sad destiny that awaited her child in Bronxville: a life of comfort and ease, free of torment, but also adventureless, a life spent always in the dining car and never on the rails. Mrs. Wister herself had wanted to be a wanderer and had dreamed once of aimless high journeys through bright Swiss mountains stopping occasionally at dusk in small villages to drink potent homemade *genever* and to sing all night with men who would admire her husky voice and strong legs. But instead she married and now drank only ginger ale and bad gin and sorrow. And so she agreed to let her child become king, but only on the condition that she could accompany and educate him. Gordon senior, whose life seemed so sure and pleasant only hours before, now watched as his wife and son marched into the pale morning fog. Do not pity him overly: This is how chance operates—quickly and cruelly. And plus, he received a nice warm scarf.

The child took a new name of his own invention, Joey Stink-Eye

Smiles. In time he sprouted to 6'9", as did his beard. As king, his duties were largely ceremonial: to open the yearly hobo convention, to maintain and raise the royal herd of corgis, to die, and then to be reincarnated. But he became much more. A vibrant and handsome young man, Stink-Eye became the closest thing the hoboes ever had to a public figure. The radio loved him, and boys' magazines built him up into a folk hero, claiming that he was a thirty-five-foot-tall lumberjack and ate one hundred pancakes a day. By the age of twenty, Stink-Eye began spinning an even taller tale—nothing less than a coup against the U.S. government: "The greatest lintwork we've ever woven," he called it. "The greatest dust storm of all."

Molly Wister Kingsmammy, as she came to be known, meanwhile grew into a revered figure herself, the godmother of the hoboes. She taught the hoboes math and cooking, and she tended to their spirits when they were sullen, which was often. Then in 1936, she was struck by a dart from the blowpipe of Walker Evans, the government agent. This was effectively the end of the hobo empire, for thereafter, Smiles gave up his coup and became obsessed with vengeance.

As the hobo wars raged across the country, Evans and Smiles hunted each other, finally meeting face-to-face in 1941 atop the Union Pacific Transcontinental train *The Final Sunset.* Their fighting shook the plains as they rumbled on, and the bloodied foes grappled still as the train roared into New York's Pennsylvania Station. Smiles's beard had been burned to a smoldering chin stump; his sixty-eight ribs were shattered; his corgis had all died defending him; and now Walker had his blowpipe aimed hard at Stink-Eye's throat as he chased him through the crowded station lobby and across its polished marble floors. But Smiles, according to hobo legend, just smiled, and disappeared into the crowd.

He was never seen again. Nor, for that matter, was any true hobo, which led the boys' magazines to speculate that Stink-Eye was never beat at all and that the fight was all a distraction. He was just buying time for the rest of the hoboes to make their final exit and escape to whatever world awaited them.

A curious epilogue: Punch, the blind hobo dog, did in fact exist. And back on that February morning in 1910, he did indeed sniff out the reincarnation of Grand Head Pipe Charles Noe—several blocks away from the Wisters. The *true* heir to the hobo throne was, it turns out, a thuggish child named Norman Boone, making Smiles's reign an incredible, if provident, error. The boy's beard, apparently, was just a coincidence.

For his part, Boone went on to tell hobo stories on the radio under the name of Boxcar Normie, though he himself never rode the rails and, despite his lineage, is considered now to be the original "faux-bo."

SEVEN HUNDRED HOBO NAMES

Though the hoboes are gone, there are those who still admire their lifestyle of unworried rambling and crusty pants. I do not understand these people and I cannot stop them. But I can insist that if you do decide to take to the rails, you should choose for yourself a proper hobo moniker. Here are seven hundred more known historical hoboes whose names you can steal. You should not feel guilty about this. If they were still at large, they would steal *your* name without hesitation. If they could manage it, they'd steal your reflection from the mirror and sell it to the still surface of a moonlit pond. And then they would drain the pond out of spite.

If you wish, you may append your hobo name with "Jr," "II," or "fils," after the custom of the more honorable hoboes, bearing in mind that the more honorable hoboes tended to be strangled on sight.

You may also use these names if you are having a child. It does not necessarily mean that they will become hoboes!

1. Stewbuilder Dennis
2. Cholly the Yegg
3. Holden the Expert Dreamtwister
4. The Rza
5. Jack Skunk
6. Jack Skunk Fils
7. Lord Dan X. Still-Standing
8. Marlon Fitz-fancy
9. Bazino Bazino, The Kid Whose Hair Is On Fire
10. Whispering-Lies McGruder
11. Nit Louse
12. Dan'l Dinsmore Tackadoo
13. Hobo Zero
14. The Silver Jacket Man
15. No-Shoulders Smalltooth Jones
16. Sistery Brothery Nabob
17. Name Withheld
18. Staniel the Spaniel
19. Frederick Bannister, the Tree Surgeon
20. Tarnose Cohen
21. Mr. Wilson Fancypants
22. Floyd Dangle
23. Shane Stoopback
24. Wicked Paul Fourteen-Toes
25. Normal-Faced Olaf
26. Tearbaby Hannity Stoop
27. The Damned Swede
28. Pierre Tin-Hat
29. Ol' Barb Stab-You-Quick
30. Mr. Whist
31. James Fenimore Cooper
32. Twistback John, the Scoliosis Sufferer
33. Sweet Daddy Champagne
34. Senator Cletus Scoffpossum
35. Horus, the Bird-Headed Fool
36. 50-Tooth Slim
37. Monk, the Monkey Man (which is to say: "the Man")
38. Thad the Bunter
39. Balloonpopper Chillingsworth
40. All-but-Dissertation Tucker Dummychuck
41. Finnish Jim

42. Flemish Jim
43. Foreign Tomas, the Strangetalker
44. Roadhouse Ogilvy and Sons
45. Jokestealer John Selden
46. Giancarlo, Master of the Metal Trapeze
47. Dr. Bill Stain-Chin, the Boxcar Medic
48. Boxcar Ted
49. Boxcar Mick
50. Boxcars [sic] Timothy Twin
51. Boxcar Jones, the Boxcar Benjamin Disraeli
52. Boxcar Aldous Huxley
53. JR Lintstockings
54. Gila Monster, Jr.
55. Irontrousers the Strong
56. "X," the Anonymous Man or Woman
57. Orphaned Reynaldo, the Child with Haunting Eyes (while there were children hoboes, Reynaldo took this name when he was 45; prior to this, he was known as . . .)
58. Reynaldo Reynaldoson, Who Will One Day Kill His Father
59. Thoughtless Harry Hsu
60. Clinical Psychiatrist Hugo Rivera
61. Peter Ox-Hands
62. Ponytail Douglas Winthrop
63. Lil' Jonny Songbird, the Songbird-Eater
64. King Snake: the Eternal Mystery
65. Ghostly Nose Silvie
66. Fonzie
67. DiCapa the Hound
68. Beef-or-Chicken Bob Nubbins
69. Honest Amelia Dirt
70. Slow Motion Jones
71. Canadian Football Pete
72. Meep Meep, the Italian Tailor
73. Jonathan William Coulton, the Colchester Kid
74. Maria the Pumpkin-Patch Crooner
75. Bix Shmix
76. Vice President Garrett Hobart
77. Stun Gun Jones
78. Prostate Davey
79. Flea Stick
80. Niles Butterball, the Frozen Turkey
81. Todd Four-Flush
82. Stick-Legs McOhio
83. The Unanswered Question of Timothy
84. Mickey the Assistant Manager
85. Guesstimate Jones
86. Goofus
87. Gallant
88. Sir Roundbelly DeDelight
89. Newton Fig
90. Chicken Nugget Will
91. Parlor Peter, the Sneak Thief
92. Ovid
93. Bathsheba Ditz
94. Alan Pockmark, Esq.
95. Lolly Hoot Holler
96. Von Skump
97. Lonnie Choke
98. Chisolm Chesthair
99. Freak Le Freak, the Freakster
100. Rex Spangler, the Bedazzler
101. Randall Mouth-Harp
102. Chrysler LeBaron
103. The Fishin' Physician
104. Persuasive Frederick
105. Celestial Stubbs
106. Teary-Eyed Fingal
107. Mairah Nix
108. Cthulhu Carl
109. Del Folksy-Beard
110. No-Banjo Burnes
111. Chainmail Giles Godfrey
112. Lois "Charles" Ladyfinger
113. Plausible Zane Scarrey
114. Huckle Smothered
115. MmmmmDandy Dundee
116. Mountain-Humper Edgar Ames
117. Spasmodic Hilary
118. Doc Aquatic
119. Molly Bewigged
120. Cincinnati O'Gurk
121. Metuchen O'Sullivan

122. Cherry Hill O'Manley
123. Cheesequake O'Lennox
124. Booper O'Montauk
125. Zaxxon Galaxian
126. Drinky Drunky Thom, the Drunk
127. Terry Gross
128. Spooky-Night Spooky Day
129. Zipgun Gloucester Gluck
130. Human Hair Frum
131. Sherlock-Holmes-Hat Carl III
132. Patrick Intergalactic
133. Ambidextrous Stang
134. Yum-Yum Sinclair Snowballeater
135. Ponzi-Scheme Jeremiah Ponzi
136. Toodles Strunk
137. Monkeybars Matthew Manx
138. Pineneedle–Jacket Jericho Fop
139. Robert the Tot
140. Robert the Child-Size
141. Robert the Minuscule
142. Robert the Wee
143. Robert Fits-in-a-Case
144. Robert Eats-for-Free
145. Robert Is-He-an-Elf? (The seven Silk brothers, all named Robert, were also known for their small stature and predictable bitterness.)
146. Dennis Big-Ear Fox
147. Jethro the Pagan
148. Asterix the Gaul
149. Black Bolt, King of the Inhumans
150. Strictly Local Henry Bobtail
151. Manny the High-Ranking Mason
152. Fry-Pan Jim Fry
153. Slo-Mo Deuteronomy
154. Half-Bearded Mark
155. Knee-Brace Kenny
156. Morris the Personal Trainer
157. Thundertwine
158. Cleats Onionpocket
159. Deformed Abe
160. Trainwhistle Abejundio
161. David No-Ears
162. Achilles Snail-Hair the Buddha

163. Frog-Eatin' Lou
164. Admiral's Club Wilbur
165. Max Meatboots the First-Class Lounger
166. Dora the Explorer
167. Ms. Mary Manx, the Tailless Cat
168. Free-Peanuts Doug
169. Steve the Human Tunneler
170. Redball Charlie Dickens
171. Twink the Reading-Room Snoozer
172. Microfiche Roy, the Side-Scroller
173. McGurk, Who May Be Found by the Card Catalogue
174. Booster D'Souza
175. Commodore Sixty-Four
176. Moped Enid, the Mopedist
177. Lamont the Junkman
178. Fast-Neck Nell
179. Bill Never-Uses-a-Cookbook
180. Bee-Beard
181. Lil' Max Meatboots
182. The Personal Secretary to Jed
183. Dee Snider
184. Sausage Patty
185. Desert Locust
186. Gummy Miles
187. Gyppo Moot, the Enigma Machine
188. Ol' Stiffpants
189. Skywise the Sexual Elf
190. Craine T. Eyebrow-Smeller
191. Lonely Heiney Alan Meister
192. Shakey Aitch the Boneyard Concierge
193. Woody Damn
194. Alatar
195. Pallando
196. Saltfish Bunyan
197. Poor, Poor, Poor Charlie Short
198. Venomous Byron
199. Five-Chambered-Stomach Mort St. John
200. Gravybelly Dunstan
201. Extra-Skin Dave
202. Beanbag-Chair Bill
203. Grant Sharpnails, the Scratcher

204. Tommy Lice-Comb
205. "Medicated Shampoo" Jonah Jump
206. General Woundwort, the Giant Rabbit
207. Genius L. Cravat, the Gentleman
208. Giant Bat Wings Roland
209. Nick Nolte
210. Salty Salty Friday
211. Fatman and the Creature
     (note: there was no creature)
212. Cecelia Graveside
213. Hoosegow Earl French
214. Stymie Stonewrist
215. Roadrunner "Meep Meep" Fabong
216. Bruised-Rib Johansson, the Beefer
217. Joachim Bat-in-Hair
218. Food-Eating Micah
219. Rubbery Dmitry, the Mad Monk
220. Honey Bunches of Donald
221. Crispy Morton
222. Feminine Forearms Rosengarten
223. Two-Headed Mike Hoover
224. Manny Stillwaggon, the Man
     with the Handlebar Eyebrows
225. Bean-Hoarder Newt
226. Texas Emil
227. The Moor of Venice
228. Averroes Nix
229. Human Hair Blanket Morris Burnes
230. Canadian Paul Tough
231. Crooner Sy
232. Manuel Pants-Too-High
233. Sylvia Patience Hidden-Forks
234. Sung, the Land Pirate
235. Opie, the Boston Bum
236. Hard-Flossing Hope Peak
237. Stingo the Bandana Origami Prodigy
238. Franklin Ape and His Inner Ear
     Infection
239. Questionable-Judgment
     Theodore Stomachbrace
240. Thermos H. Christ
241. Sir Mix-a-Lot
242. The Nine Doctor Whos
243. Lord Winston Two-Monocles

244. The Freewheelin' Barry Sin
245. Diego the Spark-Spitter
246. American Citizen Zane Pain
247. Abraham, the Secret Collector
     of Decorative China
248. Linty Sullivan, the Lint-Collector
249. Socks Monster
250. Ma Churchill
251. Pappy Churchill
252. The Young Churchill
253. The Young Churchill's Hated Bride
254. Churchill-Lover Phineas Redfish
255. Crispus T. Muzzlewitt
256. Stain-Sucker Duncan
257. Dick the Candy Dandy
258. Albuterol Inhaler Preston McWeak
259. Longtime Listener, First-Time Caller
260. Mastiff Mama
261. Tennessee Ernie Dietz
262. Sharkey, the Secret Cop
263. Gooseberry Johnson, Head Brain
     of the Hobosphere
264. Weekend-Circular Deborah
265. Marcus Chickenstock
266. Stunted Newton
267. Magnus Shortwave
268. U.S. Fool
269. Manatee the Railyard Toreador
270. Utah Manfred Succor-Munt
271. Laura Delite
272. Edwin Winnipeg
273. Eyepatch Reese Andiron
274. Tom False-Lips Real-Teeth
275. Fabulon Darkness
276. Cricket-Eating Charles Digges
277. Pally McAffable, Everybody's Friend
278. Sully Straightjacket
279. Half-Dollar Funk Nelson
280. Whitman Sampler
281. Chili-Mix Wilma Bensen
282. Sting, the Glowing Blade
283. Professor Challenger
284. Lil' Shorty Longhorn
285. Rumpshaker Phil

286. Swing State Myron
287. Alistair Crowley, the Devil
288. Gutthrower Sy Salt
289. Sweetback Barney, the Dilettante
290. The Car-Knocker Killer
291. The Chamberlain
292. The Emperor
293. The Ritual-Master
294. The Garthim-Master
295. The Scientist
296. The Gourmand
297. The Slave-Master
298. The Treasurer
299. The Scroll Keeper
300. The Ornamentalist
301. Captain Slick-Talk
302. Sackfist, the Tapdancing Trombo
303. Souvenir-Selling Mlodinow
304. Blind Buck and "Woozy," the
     Invisible Seeing-Eye Dog
305. Roundhouse Farter
306. Red Ball Pnutz
307. Fake Cockney Accent Alan Strippe
308. Air and Whiskey Dale McGlue
309. Johnny RC Airplane
310. Narcotic Morgan Suds
311. Sir Francis Drank
312. Mahayana Mike
313. Miniyana Geoffrey
314. Three-Bean Otz
315. Maury the Monsoon
316. Czech Czarlie Czill
317. Sssssssssssssssss, the Hisser
318. Thanatos Koch
319. Henry Eatsmelts
320. Modem-Sniffer Gunderson
321. Half-Albino Alejandro
322. Gluttonous-Slim
323. Ragweed-Allergic Matt
324. Amorous Luminous Dirk
325. Moray Eel Ken Elmer
326. The Railbender
327. Antonio the Ombudsman
328. Karl Solenoid IV

329. Czar King Rex the Glorious Leader
330. Andy Bunkum
331. Plastic-Moustache Mortimer Tall
332. Samuel Gel Insole
333. Lemuel Gel Insole
334. Amanda Until
335. Crispy Whiskery
336. Robert Louis Stevenson, the Pirate
337. Hobo Overload
338. Leopard Print Steven Kane
339. Astonishing Shaun Eyelash
340. Billy Creak Knees
341. Owlie
342. Anwar, the Bionic
343. Reasonably Priced Motel Reese
     Unger
344. Fibery Dana
345. Cranberry Sauce Oppenheimer
346. Nancified Frederick
347. The Loon
348. Itinerant Jane
349. Holy Hannah Hottentot-Smythe
350. Fleabottle Boone
351. Amazin' Jack Caroo
352. Stupefying P, the Riddle-Maker
353. Todd Flaky-Palms
354. Waspwaist Fritz
355. Judge Roughneck
356. Slam Dance Dooze
357. Mariah Duckface, the Beaked
     Woman
358. Count Mesmerize
359. Sonny-Boy Oedipus Acre
360. Pick Mama Susan Xavier
361. Chelsea Bacon
362. Archie Axe
363. Sally Hoot-Hoot
364. Mr. Pendleton
365. Saves-Receipts Dave
366. Sir Walter British
367. Elmer, the Crankscout
368. Golden Neck
369. Marinated Alex Pons
370. El Boot

371. Shapeshifting Demon
372. Jeremiah Tip Top
373. Amanda CeeCee Strobelight
374. Irving Alva Edison, Inventor
     of the Hobophone
375. Leather Apron
376. Lead Apron
377. Foil Apron
378. Burnt Goathead
379. Saint Sorryass
380. Overly Familiar Fung
381. Chalmers, the Bridge
     Champ
382. Elephantine McMoot
383. Neekerbeeker Perry Toenz
384. Teattime BB Stiles
385. Coalie T
386. Hubbel "I Predicted Lindy
     Hop" Deerblind
387. Hubie Hewitt, the Broadway
     Legend
388. Huge Crybaby McWeepy
389. Poo-Knickers Elias
390. Elffriend Weingarten
391. Forktongue Nigel Fork
392. Woodeye Apfel
393. Hairlip Mikhail
394. Solid First Draft Patton Taylor
395. Prettynickels, the Lamb
396. Not-Only But-Also Pete
397. Penthief Hickock
398. La Grande Mel
399. Applebee O'Bennigan
     McFridays
400. Lardy Jerry Lardo
401. Low-Carb Aleks Stovepipe
402. Hugo Stares
403. Eldred Splinters
404. Oliver, the Train-Oyster
405. Pring, Ultralord of the Hobo
     Jungle
406. Utz, the Crab Chip
407. Salt-and-Pepper Chest
408. Beverly Hills Buntz
409. Mississippi Barry Phlegm

SOME USEFUL HOBO SIGNS

The hoboes generally spoke English or other known languages. But they prized their secrecy, and more, they loved confusing others, even other hoboes. And so they would often babble in made-up tongues—a guttural, coughing, clicking, phlegmy nonsense talk called "muck-tongue" that some romantic linguists took to be actual communication, a legitimate hobo-ese, as it were. This mistake was understandable: It was not uncommon for two hoboes to have long conversations in muck-tongue, and for those conversations to lead to shouting, tears, blood, and finally passion, even though neither party knew what the other was saying.

But if they lacked a true spoken dialect, the hoboes did share a written language, a system of glyphs scrawled on barn sides and railyard fence posts left as greetings (or warnings) from one hobo to the next. The symbols themselves were crude—usually just a few chalk lines. This simplicity made them easier to recall by the road-addled mind, and largely invisible to the non-hobo.

But the alert traveler may still catch sight of a secret message that has not yet been erased by time. They draw a kind of stick-figure portrait of the hobo life, his interests, fears, and preoccupations, especially with lint:

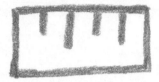

"Good source of fresh lint."

"A woman lives here who is fond of triangles."

"Great place to just mellow out."

410. Matter-Eater Brad
411. 49-State Apthorp, the Alaska-Phobe
412. New Hampshire Todd
413. "Taxachusetts" Glenn
414. Hydrocephalic Jones
415. Vermont "Greenmountain Boy" Phil Marijuana
416. Alaska Mick the Crabber
417. Arizona Ludwig
418. California Ainsley Shortpants
419. Collegeboy Brainiac, the Hobo Einstein
420. Dr. Zizmor
421. Silas Swollentoe
422. Slimneck Holden Fop
423. Aspiring Jaster
424. Illinois Obama
425. Sammy Austere
426. New Mexico Anselm Turquoise-Eater
427. Caboose-Fouling Ferris Ntz
428. Prayerful Stan, the Bent-Knee Yahoo
429. Four-Fisted Jock Socko
430. Buttery-Cheeks Anton
431. Shadow ("Blinky") Preston
432. Godigisel the Vandal
433. Gunderic Godigiselson
434. Panzo the Spiral-Cut Ham
435. Smoke-Collecting Reg
436. Hot Gnome Jimmy Jackson
437. Pontius Cornsilk-Heart
438. Sanford Who Lacks Fingerprints
439. Treesap-Covered N. Magruder
440. Thor Hammerskold, the Mexican
441. Bingo-Balls Nick Chintz
442. Bleedingtoe the Barefoot 'Bo
443. Hondo "Whatever That Lizard Is That Walks on Water"
444. Salami Sunshine

445. Fourteen-Bindlestick Frank
446. Oregon Brucie Shunt
447. Pirandello, the Many-
    Bearded
448. Quinn and His Quaker Oats
    Box Drum
449. Fatneck Runt
450. my-e-hobo.com
451. Somersaulting Mike Spitz
452. Bo 'Bo
453. Abelard "Sunken Treasure"
    Lowtrousers
454. Colin, That Cheerful Fuck
455. Battling Joe Frickinfrack
456. Monsieur Dookie, the
    Francophonic
457. Happy Horace Noosemaker
458. Hieronymous Crosseyes
459. Crumbjacket Timmy
460. Overload-the-Dishwasher
    Mac
461. Rhythmic Clyde Hopp
462. Microbrew Stymie
463. El Caballo, the Spanish
    Steed
464. Lee Burned-Beyond-
    Recognition
465. Hollering Martin Mandible
466. Damien Pitchfork, the
    Freightyard Satan
467. Handformed Hamburger
    Clarence West
468. Dr. Nobel Dynamite
469. Pickled-Noggin Nettles
470. Mischievous Craig
471. Baldy Lutz, the Amityville
    Horror
472. Ashen Merle Buzzard
473. Frypan Nonstick McGee
474. Singleminded Hubbard
475. Maryland Sol Saynomore
476. Baked Salmon Salad Finn
477. Unshakably Morose Flo
478. Fr. Christian Irish, the
    Deep-Fat Friar

"Here people tell you to go to hell."

"Hobo nickels accepted here."

*"Keep quiet, especially
about kite-flying."*

"Good flow-charts here."

"Here lives a rich man."

"Here lives a gentleman.*"*

*"The chairs in this town
are very tippy."*

*"There is an awesome
hedge maze in this town."*

479. Smokestack-Hugger Jools Nygaard
480. Fossilwise Opie Fingernail
481. Tab-Collar Dix
482. George Slay, the Duck Throttler
483. Eldon Waxhat, the Waterproof Man
484. Timely Clayton, the Human Wristwatch (so named not because of his punctuality, but because one arm was significantly shorter than the other)
485. Both Dakotas Dave
486. Duke Jeremiah Choo-Choo
487. Transistorized Maximillian, the Hobo Cyborg
488. Gravelbed Gavin Astor
489. Pantless, Sockless, Shoeless Buster Bareass
490. Alternate-Dimension Bela Boost
491. Atlas Flatshoulders
492. Scurvied Leo Falsebreath
493. Toby Anchovy, the Canned Man
494. Mad Max
495. The Goose
496. Not the Goose
497. Mister Torso, the Legless Wonder
498. Jedediah Dryasdust
499. Loving Vincent Hugsalot
500. The Rambling, Rambling Boris Wander
501. Business-Class Klaus Riel
502. Emergency Exit Aisle Gustav Nook
503. Unnervingly Candid Nicky Thain
504. Snoops Lightstep Trenchcoat, the Hobo PI
505. William Carlos Williams
506. Beef Grease Porter Dripchin
507. Exoskeleton Chester Fields

508. Roth IRA Romeo Leeds, the
     Well Prepared
509. Bum-Smiter Phillip
510. Bum-Hating Virgil Hate-Bum
511. Thor the Bum-Hammer
512. Bum-Tolerant Brendan Sleek
513. Most Agree: It's Kilpatrick
514. The Beloved Dale
     Thankyounote
515. Unpronounceable
516. Thad Malfeasance
517. Chiseltooth Muck Manly
518. Amsterdam Jocko
519. Sinister Leonard Longhair
520. Beery Clive the Eunuch
521. Chaim the Squirrelkeeper[26]
522. Nightblind and Colorblind,
     the Blind Twins
523. Milosz the Anarchist
     Puppeteer
524. Jimmy "New Man"
     Neandertal
525. Lonnie Pina Colada
526. Washington State Amy
     Swipe
527. Gopher-State Sam, the
     Minnesota Man
528. Candle-Eyed Sally
529. Packrat Red and his Cart
     o' Sad Crap
530. Trixie of the East
531. Trixie of the West
532. Fine-Nipple Tom Bazoo
533. The Friends of Reginald
     McHate Society
534. Oregon Perry Hashpipe
535. Bold 'n' Zesty Brad
536. Mermaid Betty Scales
537. Spotted Dick
538. Shanty Queen Elizabeth
     Regina
539. Nichols Crackknuckle

---

26. Please see "All Kinds of
Squirrels," p. 137.

*"Watch out! Railyard patrolled
by trained apes."*

"This house is well guarded."

"This house looks strangely familiar."

*"This house is bigger on the inside
than it is on the outside."*

"Here is a hobo trance zone."

Hoboes claimed to be able to psychically communicate in order to summon weather, signal for aid, or merely gossip, but only so long as they stood in certain natural psychic hot spots. Some have speculated that the hobo's chief desire was to visit all of these spots in the United States, with the belief that when he had done so, the hobo would be lifted up and transported to Chicken Soup Springs, aka "The Big Rock Candy Mountain." This supposed hobo Valhalla was reputed to be a beautiful, temperate land of cigarette trees and lakes of stew—two features, curiously, which astronomers now tell us are common to Uranus.

"Good sand here."

Since hoboes had the power, in sufficient number, to summon sand- and dust storms via group telepathy, good sources of sand were marked with this ideogram.

540. Stew Socksarewarm
541. Huge-Calves Dwight
542. A-Number-1
543. N-Number-13
544. Arthur Moonlight
545. Andrea Clarke, the Human Shark
546. Monkey's-Paw Patterson
547. Myron Biscuitspear, the Dumpster Archeologist
548. Ollie Ebonsquirrel
549. The Classic Brett Martin
550. Douglas, the Future of Hoboing
551. Ironbelly Norton
552. Dilly Shinguards
553. Rufus Caboose
554. Rear Admiral JF Grease Pencil
555. King Cotton
556. Prince Hal Oystershuck, the Royal Shucker
557. Unconditional Gavin
558. Squirrelcloak
559. Idaho Woody Harrelson
560. Jane the Boxcar Beekeeper
561. Aaron Three-Shirts
562. Paste-Smeller Luke
563. Lowly Highley
564. Elihu Skinpockets
565. Marian May Wyomingsong
566. Stitches the Railyard Sutureman
567. Klonopin Clyde
568. Benny Twenty-Squirrels
569. Chickeny-Flavored Remy Bunk
570. Juicepockets Thomas Moone
571. Eustace Feetbeer
572. Amnesiac Jared Stringy
573. Shagrat, Orc of the Ozarks
574. Billy Butterfly Net
575. Ammonia Cocktail Jones
576. Norma Shinynickels
577. Jonathan Crouton

"It is time for hoboes to take over the United States government."

This sign had never been seen before May 2, 1932, when it suddenly appeared on boxcars and on the doors of lint shops across the
nation, and in stranger, bolder places as well: carved into mashed
potatoes at roadside diners, chalked onto policemen's backs, and,
most famously, stamped into an Iowan cornfield on such an enormous scale that it was reputed to be seen by the president in his
Super-Copter, seventy-five feet above the earth. Hoover was said to
have been so unnerved by the sight that he dropped the giant turkey
leg he was gnawing and in a thin voice exclaimed, "So it has come:
The wandering men will kill us all." He began constructing his
pneumatic militia the very next day.

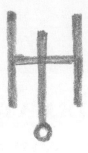

"Uranus."

This is the astrological symbol for Uranus, though it is unknown if the hoboes knew this. Discovered in 1781, Uranus upended thousands of years of common belief that the solar system terminated at Saturn, and thus it came to symbolize the breaking of old ideologies and the rejection of orthodoxy; in astrology, it is the ruling planet of occultists, inventors, and dropouts. But the hoboes may have liked it because it looked like an H, or because it sounded dirty. Nonetheless, the sudden frequency of this marking in the years following their failed coup against the United States government fueled speculation that hoboes planned and executed an actual off-world exodus to another planet.[27]

---

27. See "Hobo Matters," p. 98.

578. Antigone Spit
579. El Top-Hat Swindlefingers
580. PomPom the Texas Dancing Dog
581. Gin-Bucket Greg
582. Yuri Trimble, the Alien Pod-Person
583. South Carolina Sarah Lardblood
584. Bloody-Stool LaSalle
585. Pith-Helmet Andy
586. Self-Taught-Guitarist Edmund
587. Don Tomasino di Shit-the-Bed
588. Markansas
589. Neckfat JK Trestle
590. Pansy Overpass
591. Ralph Raclette Cornichon, Hobo of the Mountains
592. Montana Nbdego Tch!k
593. Unbearably Oenophilic Ned
594. Jonas Tugboy, Professional Masturbator
595. Cinderfella Dana Dane
596. Kerosene-Soaked Tom
597. Black-Bottle Priam
598. Pinprick Butell
599. Stool-Sample Frank
600. Iowa Noam Chomsky
601. Etienne, Roi of the Rapier
602. Amesy Squirrelstomper, the Chipmunk Preferrer
603. Ned Gravelshirt
604. NPR Willard Hotz, the Soothing-Voiced
605. Amen to Polly Fud
606. Constantly Sobbing Forrester
607. Maine-iac Leonid
608. Magnetized James
609. Hobo Jake Jerrold, Representing the Whole Mid-Atlantic Region
610. Jiminy Sinner
611. Pamela Chickeneggs (i.e., Hobo Caviar)

PART FIVE

FURTHER INFORMATION
YOU CAN USE TODAY

LYCANTHROPIC TRANSFORMATION TIMETABLES

FIFTH SEVENTH

	MINUTES AFTER MOONRISE/MOONSET		
	to-Wolf	to-Man	Transformation
Werewolf (North American)	9'24"	14'58"	full, cunning
Hombre Lobo	8'00"	9'23"	full, stealthy
Werewolf (British)	7'21"	40'21"	full, polite
Loup-Garou	7'34"	39'23"	full, wary
Varcolac	6'12"	24'21"	full, pensive
Libahunt	5'30"	22'42"	full, but has stopped killing children
Werebears and Skinwalkers	20'32"	26'23"	still rocking

CHARM POTENCY		
silver items	bullets and knives	
wolfsbane	low	
fur girdle removal	possible with mauling	
taming love of pure woman	possible with mauling	

ACTIVE

FIVE SECRETS
OF SUCCESSFUL
NEGOTIATION

I consulted several prominent, if un-named, business leaders to compile these simple, commonsense negotiating tips. If you have trouble memorizing them, picture the words in your mind. Picture them in an elegant font, and now picture them at the bottom of a cor-porate inspirational poster of the kind you see in a catalogue on an airplane, the kind that features beautiful photo-graphs of wolves or soaring eagles or golf courses. Now you will remember them. Now they are unforgettable.

1. A prominent attorney writes: "Remember that as a negotiator, you are first and foremost a mental warrior. *Think like a ninja.* But note, it is not ap-propriate to dress like a ninja." (Note: It is acceptable to dress like a samurai.)

2. A respected salesman suggests: "In any negotiation, the very first words out of your mouth should be, 'That is my final offer.' Use this starting point to then try to convince the other party that time is moving backward. Things will go much easier this way. If this gambit fails, however, you should deny ever saying anything."

615. Warbling Timmy Tin Voice and His Voicebox
616. Ambassador Roasting Pan
617. Warren Smazell, Founder of Hobotics®
618. Ventriloquism Jimmy and "Madam," the Talking Bean Can
619. Nosepicker Rick Pick
620. The Black Squirrel Fairy
621. Alabama Edsel Brainquake
622. Kid Silverhair, the Man of Indeterminate Age
623. Catscratch Tremont Nude
624. Bill Jaundice
625. Sugarhouse Morris the Sapper
626. Nutrition-Shake Emery
627. Nicknameless Norris Shine
628. Stinging Polly Papercuts
629. Deke Hidden Hornets' Nest
630. The Wisconsin Scourge
631. Brendan Headbristles
632. His Excellency Nooney Sockjelly
633. Whistling Anus Mecham, Le Petomaine
634. Talmidge, the Bactine Bearer
635. Tailstump Gunther, the Vestigial Man
636. The Hon. Charlie Weed-Farmer
637. Philatelist Joey Licks
638. Old Pliny Dance-for-Ham
639. Rheumy Sven
640. Wormy Glenn and Nootka the Flatworm
641. Hidalgo, the Devil Stick Artiste
642. The Fucky From Kentucky
643. Prince Bert in Exile, the Man in the Foil Mask
644. Siderodromophobic Billy
645. Antlered Calvin
646. Cambridge Massachusetts Claude

3. A renowned entrepreneur recommends: "Repeatedly ask to speak to the decision-maker. If the other party claims to be the decision-maker, begin intimidation technique one: silently stand, and then lift your shirt to reveal your pistol (or, alternately, your samurai sword)."

4. A bestselling author on the subject of "negotiation" reminds: "Negotiation requires compromise. Each party must gain something, and each must give something up. Before you begin your negotiation, privately consider what you are willing to give away. Now gather all of that material together and put it in a sack. Hide the sack in a secure location, such as a cave that is laced with explosives that you can detonate by remote control. Take the remote control in with you to the negotiation. As any experienced negotiator knows, in order to succeed, you must be willing to walk away from the deal at any moment, and then blow up the cave. Note: The sack should be made of velvet."

5. A former professional literary agent advises: "If you are negotiating face-to-face, be sure to separate the room first into 'power zones.' The classic five zones are: Earth, Fire, Water,

Air, and Double Scorpion. Use colored masking tape to demarcate the zones, but be sure to purify the tape first by passing it through a cloud of incense or burying it in fertile earth for five days. Cast runes to determine where your prime negotiation position is located for that day. Do not let anyone else touch your runes. Attempt to maneuver the other party into the zone that the runes favor. This is called 'getting him just where you want him.' Ignore the old adage that it is best to negotiate from a position of strength. Recent studies prove that it is always best to negotiate from double scorpion."

682. Replicant Wemberly Plastiskin and his Clockwork Squrrel "Toothy"
683. Harry Coughblood
684. Aesop Bedroll, the Fluffy Pillow Man
685. Widow-Kisser Roger
686. Experimental Hobo Infiltration Droid "41-K"
687. Baron Bayonet, the Bull-Sticker
688. Mikey Gluesniff
689. Bell's-Palsy Brennan
690. Chiptooth Berman, the Bottle Biter
691. Undertaker Robert, the Lint-Coffin Weaver
692. Betty, the Exorcist
693. Tittytwister Blake Horrid
694. Mallory Many-Bruises
695. Mad or Sad Judd (no one can tell)
696. Troglodytic Amory Funt
697. Smokehouse "Frankie" Jowl-Poker
698. Utility-Belt Deana
699. The Unshakable Will of Wade Terps
700. Trainwhistle Ernie Roosevelt, the President's Long-Lost Brother

FIGURE 18:
Ready for Negotiation

HOW TO WIN A FIGHT

Sometimes, sadly, negotiation fails, and that is when fighting begins. I am not exactly proud to report that I do have some experience in this field as well.

For while I am now a very quiet person who rarely leaves his home, it is true that when I was a Professional Literary Agent, I was involved in many fights, as well as several imbroglios and two major feuds, and throughout all of these conflicts, I was always the victor. I am basically unbeatable. I don't mean to boast, but whether it is a fistfight, a test of wills, or psychic combat, I always seem to win, and people naturally want to know how this can be. The answer is very simple, and I am pleased to share it with you now: I have a *system for winning.* And it has three steps.

STEP 1: ALWAYS MAKE EYE CONTACT. If you turn away, you show fear. Even if your enemy is not in the same room, you should always be making eye contact, preferably for an hour or longer. Once you have made eye contact for twenty-five minutes or so, go ahead and raise one eyebrow. This is very intimidating. You may have noticed that Dwayne Johnson, the wrestler and actor known as "The Rock," uses this trick all the time. And in fact, I taught him how to do it when he was visiting my private island in 1997.

STEP 2: GO AHEAD AND USE HENCHMEN. I know everyone wants to fight his own battles, but in this day and age, it is simply unnecessary and actually sort of frowned upon. Especially when there are so many skilled henchmen who are out of work. I also recommend buying your henchmen satin jackets with a picture of your face embroidered on the back. My feeling is that if it is good enough for the Joker, it should be good enough for you.

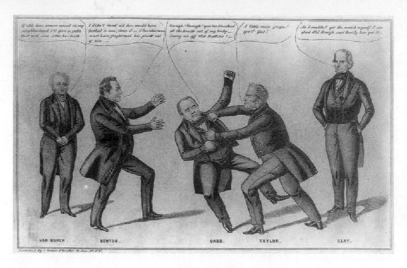

FIGURE 19: *Historical Fisticuffs*

STEP 3: I CANNOT STRESS THIS ENOUGH: RUN LOTS OF ATTACK ADS. This has always worked for me. Some people say that these ads are just negative smears and bad for our country. I say that those people have voted to raise taxes ninety-five times and are probably from Massachusetts. In fact, a certain magazine recently ranked those people the number-one "most incorrect" and "probably gay" people in Massachusetts, and the number-one "most personally against" John Hodgman. So who are you going to trust? Me? Or the probably gay Massachusetts residents who are against me?

I have run about five hundred attack ads this year, and I expect that I will buy even more air time next year, because my enemies are getting stronger. As a template for your own efforts, I am happy to provide for you here, for the first time in print, the scripts of three of my most successful attack ads.

ATTACK AD #1

"Borderline irresponsible . . ."

That's what friends of John Hodgman are saying about Jonathan Coulton.

Last weekend, Jonathan Coulton agreed to look in on John Hodgman's cats when he was in Montreal.

The fact is: He didn't. Even though the record shows that Coulton has his own cat, so he obviously knows how to take care of one.

Something just doesn't add up.

Cat out of the bag, Mr. Coulton?

John Hodgman is a better choice. When John Hodgman found a stray cat on 105th Street last week, he worked tirelessly to find it a home.

He even took it to the vet for a checkup.

Fact is, John Hodgman is working hard for cats: *all cats.* Not just the ones he owns.

"Borderline irresponsible . . ."

"Doesn't add up . . ."

"Cat out of the bag . . ."

Does Jonathan Coulton sound like someone you want to cat-sit for you?

Henrietta Pussycat says, "Meow meow meow meow, *NO WAY,* meow meow meow."

I ran this next ad a few years ago when I was taking a former sub-letter of mine to court for not paying his back rent, which I then had to pay.

ATTACK AD #2

What's going on with Felipe Oliveira?

When John Hodgman needed a subletter for his apartment, Oliveira said he was the man for the job.

But his résumé tells a different story.

Turns out, Oliveira was not just a local waiter, but also a Portuguese hypnotist.

Say what?

And it turns out, Felipe Oliveira also goes by the name PHIL MOORE.

Run that by me again?

What Oliveira doesn't want you to know is that when he skipped out on $1,200 worth of back rent, Hodgman's landlord described Oliveira as a "deadbeat" and said that Oliveira had been caught masturbating out of the window *on two separate occasions.*

Cat out of the bag, Mr. Oliveira?

John Hodgman is a better choice. He has never practiced hypnosis, never used an alias, and has masturbated out of a window only once.

Deadbeat . . .

Masturbator . . .

Hypnotist . . .

Grant John Hodgman a summary judgment against Mr. Oliveira and let him move on with his life.

After all, it's time to reach out and unite our country. Not *masturbate out a window.*

And here is another, an ad I ran in the Saratoga Springs, New York, area just after my wife and I were married.

ATTACK AD #3

Seven hundred dollars.

That's how much the Delia Hotel in Saratoga demanded as a deposit to cater John Hodgman's wedding in 1999.

Seven hundred dollars.

That's how much it cost to reserve the main dining room, which the Delia Hotel said could hold two hundred people.

Fact is, the Delia would be lucky if the dining room could hold one hundred people.

Fact is, *the Delia lied,* and when John Hodgman asked for his deposit back, the Delia Hotel suddenly stopped returning his calls.

Seven hundred dollars.

Is that the going rate . . . *for a swindle?*

Seven hundred dollars.

Or is that money the Delia needs to continue to house a coven of evil witches?

Small . . .

Greedy . . .

Doesn't return phone calls . . .

The Delia Hotel: is it full of *witches?*

I hope this has proved instructive. Naturally, these messages have been paid for by the Friends of John Hodgman, and they have been approved by me, John Hodgman.

SHORT WORDS FOR USE ON SUBMARINES TO PRESERVE OXYGEN

See Table 13, page 134.

TABLE 13: "SWUSPOs"	
"COB"	Chief of the Boat.
"Cockions"	Cocktail onions. A favorite snack among sub-mariners, as they make no noise when eaten.
"Con"	Control of the subma. Under COTU, he who has "the con" need not relinquish it until he is ready. Thereafter, "the con" automatically goes to Nemo or whomever has put a quarter on the screen.
"COTU"	Code of the Underseas: an unofficial and unwritten code of sub-mariner conduct. While some precepts are universally accepted (i.e., "a sub-mariner never climbs a mountain"; "a sub-mariner who kills a merman shall raise that merman's children"; "a sub-mariner never opens the windows"), others are simply made up on the spot in an effort to confuse JAFOs ("a senior sub-mariner has the right to confiscate all hidden diamonds belonging to a junior sub-mariner").
"Counsie"	The staff Creative Writing Counselor.
"Dern"	Any sub-mariner who is seen by his colleagues to embody the poignant fortitude of the Bruce Dern character in the science-fiction film *Silent Running*.
"DoNoWeSh"	Do not wear shoes. A common general order when the hoagie is SR.
"DoppelCOB"	The chief of the boat's identical twin brother (archaic). Identical twins were considered to be good luck aboard early undersea vehicles, and were often placed in positions of authority so as to intimidate unruly sailors by seeming to be in several places at once. To this end, and also because it was amusing, they usually dressed alike. USN prohibited identical twin brothers from traveling on the same submarine after the Feeney tragedy, when the US sub *Hidden Meaning* was crushed by a GSOL in 1953. The COB, Mike Feeney, was only fourteen years old when he succumbed to the creature's powerful tentacles and/or claws. By horrible coincidence, his identical twin brother and DoppelCOB, Doug Feeney, also died that very day, on the same doomed submarine, while wearing the same clothes.

TABLE 13: "SWUSPOs" *continued*	
"GSOL"	Giant Squid Or Lobster. Passive sonar is notoriously unable to distinguish between these two creatures. A dangerous indistinction, as the giant squid is a peaceful creature that is also delicious.
"Hot Bunk"	A general order for sub-mariners to sit on one another's laps.
"JAFO"	Just Another Fucking Oxygen-breather. A rookie sub-mariner.
"Nemo"	The ship's captain, also known as "the Sikh" or "the Great Scientist."
"SO"	Screech Owl. Because the screeching was easily detected by the sonar of enemy submarines, these once-favored pets are no longer allowed on submarines. This word has now come to mean any contraband.
"SR"	Silent Running. A general call for silence on a submarine when it is attempting to evade enemy sonar. Named after the sub-mariners' favorite movie.
"Sub"	This term is frowned upon by seasoned submarine personnel ("sub-mariners"). Instead say "subma" or "hoagie."
"SuDs"	Surface Dwellers. Despised.
"US Gravy"	A sub-mariner's paycheck.
"USN"	United States Navy.
"US NAVY"	*UnderSea NAVigational Yew:* a forked branch, traditionally of yew, used as a divining rod to help the submarine find water.
"Zeps"	Zeppelins, and/or members of an airship crew. Both are loathed by all sub-mariners, who feel that the zeps are just copying them, except in the air. Like "sub," "zep" also refers to a sandwich of meat and cheese on either a long Italian roll or French bread. Do not order one on a hoagie, or you will be shunned for the rest of the voyage.

SOME AMERICAN TELEPHONE NUMBERS
BEGINNING WITH "666"

666-3829—An unfortunate Bible college in Kentucky that many think is an urban legend, proving once again: many are wrong.

666-4850—A normal-looking house that, on closer inspection, has no right angles.

666-0098—An independent copier toner salesman who regularly drinks the coffee he left on his desk the day before.

666-2103—Devil worshippers who got lucky.

666-3682—Refuses to get caller ID.

666-4709—They always answer promptly, but speak no known human language.

666-8138—The author's home telephone number.

ALL KINDS OF SQUIRRELS

I am not romantic about squirrels. Long ago, when I was younger, I had the opportunity to spend many afternoons wandering about Hyde Park in London. There are many things for an unemployed youth to admire in this, one of England's largest and most vermin-filled parks, including the world-famous Speaker's Corner, the Marble Arch, the Rotten Row, and of course men feeding the many fat squirrels and pigeons who reside there.

They would hold their hands aloft, and pigeons would alight there, and squirrels would scamper up and down their legs and shoulders and arms. This seemed like honorable and adventurous work at the time, and so I decided to give it a try. The next day, I outfitted myself with a loaf of bread and loose-fitting, scamper-friendly clothing and held out my crumb-filled hand.

There were some things I had not anticipated.

First, I had not anticipated that this hobby would be so scratchy and uncomfortable. When one sees illustrations of Saint Francis, the beast-lover, bedecked all over with loving bluebirds and titmice and raccoons and such, it looks inspiring. You might even imagine that all those little paws at work upon your body might actually improve your circulation.

It is different, though, when you have a dozen pigeons clamoring to sink their clawed feet into your neck and head. Pigeons are heavier than you might think, and many are deformed, especially around the feet.[28]

This was unpleasant. But it was the squirrel that made me rethink the whole endeavor. It was the size of a terrier, and it crawled up my leg with patient greed, weighing at the fabric with its awful, furred bulk. I looked down into its face, its contemptuous eyes, and its teeth: yellow, crisscrossed, and sharp. This was not a pleasant rodent but a desperate devourer. I fed it, and I felt dirty—mainly because it had left a trail of shit and grime up my pants from its claws. But not only for this reason.

---

28. Please see "Lobster-Claw v. Pigeon-Foot Deformities," p. 142.

FIGURE 20: *A Despicable Habit*

As I looked up and saw the other vermin feeders around me, I saw that their pants were dirty as well, but in different, disturbing ways. And for the first time I saw that many of these men had beards, and that their beards were often unkempt and often had strange objects lodged in them. These were not just animal-loving retirees. How had I not noticed it before? They were basically hoboes! And I was becoming one of them.

I had seen in that squirrel's face a kind of hard truth that I still don't like to admit: nature is ravenous. If you are not careful, it will either consume you or transform you into its twisted servant. And so at that moment, I shrugged the remaining animals off my shoulders and body (a process that took about twenty-five minutes). I threw my remaining bread in one direction and fast-walked on shaky legs in the other and did not look back.

Some years later, though, I saw another squirrel. I had returned to New York, and had taken to eating my lunch in Madison Square, a small park near the Flatiron Building. It was a spring afternoon, and suddenly my squirrel scratches began to throb, as they always do when one of those creatures draws near. But this particular one was entirely new to me. It was jet black, small and lithe, a scampering dark shadow on the green grass. Like any rational person, I presumed it was an omen that I would die within a week.

But a week passed, and when I did not die, and instead saw only more and more black squirrels all over the city, I resolved to investigate.

After some reading, I learned that black squirrels are actually quite common in the American Midwest—especially in Council Bluffs, Iowa, and Marysville, Kans., which are the twin epicenters of American black squirreldom. And lately, the hearty species has been on the move, gradually radiating toward the coasts. Some speculate they are driven by deforestation. Every schoolchild knows that a squirrel could once run from Greenland to Cuba on a canopy of trees and perhaps now they are intent on taking it back, overrunning us as indeed all nature will someday. And so at least in this sense, the omen of the black squirrel is true. But I also don't think we should discount the encouragement of those squirrel-feeders I observed in London. One wonders what secret agenda they and their ilk might hold as they literally fuel the squirrels' dreadful scamper across our land.

TABLE 14: ALL KINDS OF SQUIRRELS

Type	Habitat	Skills
Eastern Gray	Originating in Eastern Canada and the United States, it has now spread throughout the world by a combination of natural guile and the manipulation of old and eccentric men, who seem hypnotically bound to feed them.	Despite its thuggish bulk, the Eastern Gray has a sharp and pitiless mind well-adapted to scientific research. Its greatest accomplishment is the development of the dreaded Parapox virus, which it has used successfully to largely eliminate its rival, the Eurasian Red, in much of the Red's former territory.
Eurasian Red	Coniferous forests throughout Europe; a hidden valley in Nepal.	With its ruddy coat and handsome ear tufts immortalized in countless illustrated children's books, this was the default squirrel for most European children until the Eastern Gray began its scurrying march across the Old World. The reds initially fought back, but they always had a different temperament from the gray invaders, and their resistance via impassioned essays and street theater proved a fruitless defense against all the clawing and biting. Not to mention the Parapox virus. Eventually they were forced to retreat to remote Asia, their ancestral half-homeland, where they are now concentrating on creating a perfect society, one where the artist shall be revered and the poet shall govern. Naturally this shall fail.
American Red	Across Canada and the U.S. as far south as Appalachia.	Commonly referred to as "The Unfaithful" or "Those Who Did Not Heed the Call" for failing to come to the aid of their threatened European cousins, but the American Reds consider themselves a peace-loving species and would like you to consider other factors—their beneficial seed dispersal, their consumption of mushrooms that are poisonous to humans, their loveable prancing—before you condemn them in your hearts.
Bronze	Dwells in shallow seas and occasionally enters lagoons, where it will sometimes surface to speak to passing adventurers.	Highly intelligent and known for its riddle-making, the Bronze Squirrel breathes lightning and repulsion gas.

TABLE 14: ALL KINDS OF SQUIRRELS *continued*

Type	Habitat	Skills
White/Albino	Two American towns compete for the honor and tourist dollars of being the "white squirrel capital" of the U.S.—Olney, Ill., and Marionville, Mo. Though Marionville may claim more of these genetic oddities in raw numbers, Olney counters that it is home to more *true* albino squirrels. But both populations are fragile—numbering in the low hundreds at best. In order to preserve them, both towns have strict leash laws, and Marionville went so far as to ban dogs and cats altogether. Olney, fearing white flight, not only followed suit, but also extended the ban to all cars, and transformed the town's public lands into a "Habitrail Necklace" of connected plastic tubes and nesting stations. Marionville, in response, actually outlawed all other squirrels, paying $10 a head to any child who presents the body of a nonwhite squirrel, no questions asked, and destroying the home of any person who harms a white squirrel, even by accident. It is difficult to predict which approach will be more effective in luring the white squirrel, who is notoriously fickle, and mainly looking for tax breaks.	They are white.
Flying	Known as the fuzzy-tailed rats of the air, flying squirrels inhabit the skies of most of North America and Europe, feeding on hawks, eagles, and sky nuts. They rarely land, instead sleeping briefly as they glide earthward in great circles or, more recently, hitching rides on airplanes.	Their gigantic, clawed wings were the inspiration for da Vinci's sketches of a prototype flying machine/squirrel costume.
Black	Whereas legend suggests that the white squirrels were first brought to the U.S. by a band of gypsies, it is certain now that the black squirrels were brought by the hoboes. Favored as pets and confidants, they were used to carry messages within the hobo jungle and given honored burial when they died. When the hoboes disappeared in the 1940s, they left their squirrels at the crossroads—the great rail junctions at Council Bluffs, Iowa, and Marysville, Kans. But the squirrels were not completely abandoned, for before leaving the hoboes had hypnotically instructed the tramps and bums to care for the squirrels. Today those who have ever tasted wanderlust or hobo envy cannot long resist the desire to feed a squirrel, black or no (indeed, that is the legacy I discovered in London). Over time the black squirrels gained in strength and number. Some believe that when the hoboes are ready, the squirrels will return to the road, migrating to every part of the land to await their masters' return.	Their harsh clicking and scolding is considered musical by some, but they are best known for their excellent memories and unwavering discretion. As hoboes disdained memory, it fell to the squirrels to keep their secrets and to recall the combinations to their many hidden dirt safes.

LOBSTER-CLAW V. PIGEON-FOOT DEFORMITIES

It is not uncommon in roadside restaurants in the state of Maine to see a display of strange lobster claws that have been found by local fishermen. Nearly fifty million lobsters are taken out of the water each year in Maine, so it is not statistically surprising that some number of these will have what I would term in polite company an "effed-up claw," and one may appreciate why these might tempt an enterprising person to collect, dry, and display them on a plaque. Because, as every restaurant owner knows, if you horrify children, they will come back again and again.

Pigeons, as I have pointed out, also suffer from frequent deformities of the claw, which is called by experts "the foot." But these are less often displayed on plaques because they are smaller and more difficult to preserve, and far more disgusting. Still, the curious person cannot help but wonder how they stack up against each other.

TABLE 15: LOBSTER-CLAW V. PIGEON-FOOT DEFORMITIES		
Lobster	**Pigeon**	**Advantage**
The double claw	The two-toed foot	Lobster
The pretzel claw	The twenty-toed foot	Pigeon
The claw shaped like the body of a bumblebee	The foot that cannot really be called a foot	Lobster
The claw that resembles the skyline of Portsmouth, N.H.	The foot that has an extra pigeon at the end of it	Lobster
The claw whose teeth spell out in Braille: "I shall be avenged"	The feet that look like little human hands	Pigeon

Results: The lobster claw gains a slight edge for offering the more varied and, at times, poetic deformities. But the pigeon foot must be credited for reminding us, often to the point of nausea, that we are but flesh, accidentally formed.

SECRETS OF YALE UNIVERSITY

As a graduate of this fine and mysterious institution, I am glad, as always, to clarify a few of your misconceptions and to confirm even more of your suspicions.

SECRET!: Yale was built by Elihu Yale with his own hands out of mud.
STATUS: Somewhat true

Yale was *not* built by this person, but the institution that would eventually become the university was founded in 1701 as the "Friends of Elihu Yale." This was a social club of prominent south-

FIGURE 21: *Skull and Bones—No Threat to the Secret World Government*

ern Connecticutians that was devoted to drinking and the display of friendship to Elihu Yale, a Boston-born merchant living in England whom they had chosen at random.

The Friends of Yale would secretly meet every Thursday evening to plan out lavish new gifts for Mr. Yale—teams of horses, some carved out of gold; chests of tobacco and guns; magic cotton gins; a wise prostitute who would remind Yale of the brevity of life and its beauty, etc.—all shipped, at great expense, to Yale, who did not want them and did not know why he was receiving them.

"Unknown gentlemen," he wrote in 1718, "whether it is your aim to display great charity or great malice cannot be clear, but I urge you please to stop. I have already married the prostitute, and I cannot by law take another chest of nutmeg." He instead urged them to accept money to establish "Such a School that shall be Useful to the Local Youths of Quality to teach them the principles of godliness and Secret World Government." And thus, Yale was born.

One possible explanation of the rumor stated above is the fact that, while Yale was not actually made of mud, the entire campus *was* buried under the earth for ten years to make it appear older.

SECRET!: The world is secretly controlled by Skull and Bones.
STATUS: Not true at all. NOT AT ALL.

I should like to say for the record I am not a "Bonesman" or indeed a member of any of the exclusive "senior societies"—Book and Snake, Scroll and Key, Snake and Eggs, the Leatherstockingmen, the Yale School of Forestry, etc. Due to their open advocacy of cloak-wearing and their great windowless clubhouses known as "tombs" (many of them carved out of a single block of marble), these societies have prompted much fanciful speculation about bizarre masturbation rituals and hidden plans for world domination.

It is true that all of the past fourteen presidential candidates have been Bonesmen, with the exception of Ralph Nader, who was merely a member of the much less prestigious consumer-advocacy society Scroll and Seatbelt. And it is also true that Skull and Bones was originally chartered by the Illuminati and Knights Templar in order to *infiltrate* the Secret World Government at Yale's New Haven campus. But having failed to make any progress in this goal, the Bonesmen now focus almost exclusively on tending to the pterodactyls on their private island and on ritual masturbation.

SECRET!: Yale enforces its will on the world via a capella singing groups.
STATUS: Absolutely true.

While many of Yale's sixty-odd a capella singing groups are merely social organizations, a handful compose the Secret World Government's most trusted and elite forces; generally their expertise breaks down thusly:

The Whiffenpoofs	—conventional espionage, fencing, suicide missions
The Spizzwinks	—traditional safecracking, now also encompassing computer espionage and movie/TV trivia
The Alleycats	—sleight of hand, small arms, seduction
The Duke's Men	—the kicking and punching of people
The Society of Orpheus and Bacchus	—counterfeiting and forgery
Tangled Up in Blue	—codes and ciphers
The Hodgmans	—the singing of beautiful songs without accompaniment

SECRET!: Sterling Memorial Library holds a book in which is predicted the fate of the United States through the year 3000.
STATUS: More true than not.

The *Americanomicon* technically is held in the miniature version of that great library that can be found on the normal-sized library's roof.[29] The Yale Lock Company was created to protect the book, securing it with special padlocks that can only be opened with *a key*. That said, it is fairly common for enterprising students to sneak up and view it at least once. I myself have held it in my hands. It is pretty mildewy.

SECRET!: The first submarine was invented at Yale and still patrols its underwater canals.
STATUS: True.

Yale graduate David Bushnell's one-man submersible, called the *Turtle*, was first deployed in New York Harbor in 1775. Piloted and powered by the volunteer Ezra Lee, the *Turtle*'s underwater crossbows cleared the harbor of all British ships as well as their trained sea-lions-of-war. Lee eventually became a member of the U.S. Secret Service under direct supervision of Yale. Though Lee did not complain about the *Turtle*'s notoriously cramped conditions, he many years later committed suicide by stuffing himself into a hatbox.

SECRET!: The Whiffenpoofs stole the Hope Diamond and presented it to Dick Cavett when they were guests on his television program in 1970.
STATUS: False.

It was the crystal skull of Alexander Hamilton.

SECRET!: Every year one student is randomly assigned to live in an extremely luxurious room made of solid gold.
STATUS: True.

---

29. Please see "Two Libraries That Are Smaller Than This Book," p. 53.

The Vanderbilt Suite, built for the son of Cornelius Vanderbilt, comprises fourteen golden rooms of pure luxury, including five-inch carpets, canopy beds in every room, a direct pipeline to the Hathorn #1 Spring in Saratoga Springs, a butler's palace, three walk-in fireplaces, the state's first electric brandy decanter, a dedicated proxy to perform all classwork, and a topographical map of the United States with a gigantic model train set that shows the real-time progress of every train currently riding the rails.

SECRET!: Yale is the seat of the Secret World Government.
STATUS: True.

There is no Secret World Government.

DEBATED PLANETS

Many of what we term "planets" have been observed since antiquity, beginning especially with the Mesopotamians, those dreamers. But especially since the discovery of Uranus in 1781, there has been resistance to admitting new bodies into the "Club of Planets."

The Club of Planets, as you know, is headquartered in a town house on East Fifty-first Street in New York City. Its charter maintains that serious people will withhold final judgment until a body's planethood may be personally verified by a visit from a club representative. Thus Saturn, Earth, and Venus are currently listed as "Undeniable Planets." But several others remain up for debate. For example . . .

PLUTO: Some scientists now consider this to be a remote planetoid of the Kuiper Belt.

SEDNA: A recently discovered body of ice and rock, most agree this is not a planet but part of the Oort cloud at the edge of the solar system. It is believed that the Oort cloud is the source of all comets, though no comet factories have yet been observed.

URANUS: Is it a planet, or just a bit of hobo myth?

NEPTUNE: The residents of its thirteen moons believe reli-
giously that Neptune itself doesn't exist. When they purify it
from their minds, the "Great Blue Insult" shall disappear.

JUPITER: Possibly just a moon of the largest planet, Gigantor.

SUPER-GIGANTOR: A hypothetical mass designed to annoy
Jupiter.

MARS: Probably a government conspiracy.

MERCURY: Zero axial tilt? Please. Most agree that this is either
a space station or a self-aware supercomputer.

Postscript: since the Club Verification Committee verified Saturn
and Venus via rocket expedition in 1959 and 1967, respectively, each
has been granted its own room in the Club of Nations: The Solarium
is now called the Saturnium; The Hall of Venus is on the third floor,
left of the Game Room, and is, in deference to the Venutians, kept at
roughly 500 degrees Celsius.

COMMON SHORT AND LONG CONS

Many con men who once prowled the hotel bars and cruise liners in
search of an easy mark now trawl the Internet for gullible souls. They
write e-mails pretending to be Nigerian Vicodin salesmen, for example, who need your credit card information to authorize your free
pornography. (This is an old and artless scam. Long before the World
Wide Web it was circulated by telegraph, which is how I was first
stung. It was, in fact, the last message carried by the Pony Express.)
    But a few old-style grifters still practice the vanishing, intimate

art of the close-up con. Traditionally they will attempt to recruit a mark into stealing from a third party (or from the grifter himself), thus making it less likely that the mark, when taken, will call the police. "You cannot cheat an honest man" goes the old con-man saying, and that is why most con men still carry polygraphs.

Some classic cons, like "The Thieving Ferret," may take just a moment ("Let's use my ferret to steal that diamond. All I need is a little seed money to get him out of the kennel.") In other schemes, such as "The Spanish Prisoner" or "The Portuguese Hypnotist,"[30] it may take weeks or months to develop the trust required to truly fleece a fellow citizen. "The Decline of the Full Service Department Store and the Advent of Big Box Retailing," in fact, requires 250 shills and ten years to pull off successfully. Against this sort of criminal dedication, the mark has little chance and, once conned, but one recourse: to con the con man.

Gradually training yourself over many years in the art of the grift, slowly gaining the trust of the criminal community, and gradually becoming your enemy so that you may finally crush him or her with one final, ultimate swindle is called "Chuckling the Kingboy" and is considered to be the greatest con of all. But before you attempt it, you should review the following basic cons. And please make sure that it is legal to keep a ferret in your native state, or else it will all end very badly for you.

PIG IN A POKE

This is a centuries-old scam in which the mark believes he is buying a delicious suckling pig in a burlap sack (a common enough suckling pig delivery device). When he opens it, however, he will find that the wriggling "poke" instead contains only a disgusting cat. Generally the cat will then flee, leaving the mark "holding the bag," as they say. But sometimes the cat (who is always in on the scheme, no matter how much he yowls) will not run and instead will

---

30. Please see "How to Win a Fight," p. 129.

try another con on the already bewildered mark—usually the old "Milk-and-Saucer Game," or the "Vomit Fake-out."[31] Since most Americans nowadays find live suckling pigs equally as distasteful as cats, more often the bag is said to contain cheap prescription drugs or an angry ghost.

THE PAJAMA MAN

The mark is approached late at night outside a bar by a shoeless man wearing only his pajamas. The pajama man claims to be a somnambulist.

"I wake up all the time like this," he will say. "But *this* is new." He will show the mark a large bundle of cash and/or some jewels. He will seem distraught. "I do not know how I got it!"

The pajama man will ask the mark to hold the money for him—if there's any police investigation, no one will think to ask the mark about it. Then when the heat is off, the pajama man will split the haul with the mark as payment for his trouble. Most of the money is counterfeit, and the jewels are paste. But it doesn't matter. If the mark takes the bait, the pajama man will thank him profusely and offer to buy him a drink. They will go back into the bar.

As they talk, the pajama man will muse, "I am a normal person in the daytime, but when I sleep, I must be some kind of a master cat burglar."

The mark will think about this in silence. He will think of his wife's valuable collection of porcelain figurines, or the bearer bonds in his asshole partner's office, or the safe in the basement of the home of his spinster aunts.

"Say," the pajama man will say, "you're doing *me* a favor. How about I do you one?"

The next night, the mark and the pajama man will meet in front the mark's office, or the mark's own home, or that of his aunts. He

---

31. Please see the asterisked note to "How to Write a Book: The Fifty-Five Dramatic Situations," p. 44, for an example of this in action.

will tell the pajama man exactly where to find the goods, and the pajama man will close his eyes, to let the information "seep into his unconscious mind."

FIGURE 22: *"Let's Use My Ferret to Steal That Diamond . . ."*

Then the pajama man will settle in behind a nearby bush or fence to fall asleep, and the mark will return to the bar to drink and joke loudly and establish an alibi. He will imagine the pajama man rising, trancelike, from his hiding place, shimmying up a drainpipe or silently forcing a back door. Tomorrow, the mark believes, he will meet the pajama man and divvy the spoils. The mark is confident of this. But then, that is confidence for you.

THE LENNY AND SQUIGGY

The mark is approached by a man who claims to have been robbed. He is especially upset because the robbers stole his entry fee for a celebrity impersonator contest. He will show the mark a hand-bill advertising the contest: a $10,000 cash prize is to be paid to the best impersonators of Lenny and Squiggy from the television program *Laverne & Shirley*.

The mark will ask if the man is himself a celebrity impersonator.

"Of course not," the con man will say, laughing. "I don't look like Lenny *or* Squiggy." And the mark will silently agree. The con man will explain that he is the *manager* of a Lenny-and-Squiggy impersonation team, and he is staking them to the contest. "These boys will go far," the con man will say.

He will show the mark a photo of his "clients." Of course, it's a publicity photo of the actual Lenny and Squiggy that has been altered with a computer to make it look like the two "impersonators" are having dinner with the con man at a local steakhouse.

"Don't get me wrong, the boys will be crushed if they can't compete," the con man will say. But that's showbiz. That's not why he's upset. He's not a sentimentalist. "It's easy enough to find a Lenny *or* Squiggy. But to get both . . ." The con man will just shake his head sadly. "That's real money. The chance of a lifetime."

"Of course," the con man will explain. "I can probably raise half the entry fee by the deadline, which is tonight. But where am I going to get the rest?"

Then he will wait for the mark to suggest the inevitable. The mark will loan him the money, in exchange for part of the winnings.

"I can't let you do it," the con man will say. "You don't even know me." And at this point the mark, inevitably, will already be nursing second thoughts. They will both mull it over for a bit—the mark sincerely, the con man theatrically.

And anyway, the con man will say, he's not sure the boys will go for it. "Let's get Squiggy on the phone and ask him." The con man will then place a phone call and have a long conversation explaining that they may have a new partner coming in, and how would Squiggy feel about that? The con man will listen, grimacing, and then hand the phone over. "He wants to speak to you," he will say.

The mark will take the phone and put it to his ear. "Who are you?" the nasal voice on the other end will say. "Who are you?" The mark will be speechless: He will hear the living voice of Squiggy. It will be absolutely uncanny. He will hurry off the phone and quickly close the deal, forking over the cash he will never see again, never realizing that the voice on the other end was not a Squiggy impersonator at all, but the actual Squiggy, the actor David L. Lander. Of course the con man has no real relationship with him, but his telephone number is easier to get than Michael McKean's.

Meanwhile, David L. Lander, who still works as he continues to struggle with multiple sclerosis, will hang up the phone, bewildered for the third time this week, and he will ponder the strange price of fame.

THREE-CARD MONTE

The mark is lured into a street-corner game of chance by a man with three cards. This man is Monte. The mark is shown the cards, one of which is the queen of hearts. They are then turned facedown on a table and moved around. The mark will be asked to locate the queen. For the first few rounds, his guesses will be correct. A small crowd will gather. They will be amazed at his skill.

Then the mark will be asked to wager some amount of money. If he hesitates, another observer will take the bet and win. Big-time: fifty bucks becomes a thousand in his hand. "One thousand sweet dollars," the other player will say, counting the crisp new bills he has won. He will look at the mark. "How can you turn this down?" he will say. He will flatter the mark, pointing out that all his guesses have been correct so far. And the mark will know it is true—that could have been *his* thousand dollars, had he only bet.

More cards will slide across the table. "Ladykiller! You know where the lady is!" the other player will say heartily. And the mark does. He is sure of it. "Look at you," the other player will say. "You're a sharp character. I'm betting with you. You've got clean trousers. You've got the cleanest trousers here."

The mark will not know what this means, but at last he will relent. He will bet small. The other observer says, "Yeah! I bet with him. A hundred dollars!" The mark will raise his bets. The sun will go behind a cloud. "Yeah!" says the other observer, clapping his back. "Mister Clean-Trousers!"

Monte will reach to turn over the chosen card. Needless to say, he has confederates. The other player, of course, is a shill, one of several among the crowd, at this moment picking the mark's pockets. He will get a kickback, as will the table, which is actually a man in a table suit, ready to flee at the first sign of the police; as will the coworker of the mark, who asked him to pick up a sandwich at a certain sandwich shop on the way back to the office, knowing that the mark would pass the game on the way and be intrigued; as will the psychologist who devised the distracting term "clean-trousers."

Also, the cards themselves are coated in Vaseline. But this is invisible to the mark, who will watch as the final card is turned. It will not be a queen. It will, strangely, look like a photo of the mark, but it will be hard to tell, for it will instantly turn into a bat, which will screech and flutter, distracting the mark as the money is swiftly picked up and divided. The man in the table suit rises and sprints around the corner. The confederates light firecrackers and disappear in the bang and the smoke, and Monte goes with them.

THE VENGEFUL NINJAS

A woman ninja approaches a mark in a railroad station and claims to be a traveling salesperson, specializing in herbal medicine. She is beautiful, and she shows him the herbal medicine, so why should the mark doubt the story?

As they speak, the ninja will confess to being *nukenin*, a rogue ninja who left her ninja village without authorization. Certainly the mark will know that the punishment for this is death.

She will go on to explain that there are several vengeful ninjas hunting her even now, and she will discreetly draw the mark's attention to the three among the crowd of ordinary travelers, who are even now observing, waiting to catch her alone.

These people will be selected at random, of course. They will not be ninjas at all. But ninjas are known for their extraordinary tale-spinning skills. And suddenly, the satin-jacketed man buying the lottery ticket at the newsstand, the obese child eating corn on the cob with great intensity,[32] and the frail, elderly man whom the mark had previously thought should not be traveling alone . . . they all seem suspicious. How many of them are stealthy warriors? How many have sworn by the code of *ninpo*?

The mark will ask the woman ninja why she does not simply disappear or summon a giant toad to aid her as is the ninja way. She will say that those are just myths.

At this point she will call the mark by his first name. He does not remember telling it to her. "Mark," she says (let's say that is his name), "as long as I am alone, I will be at risk. Will you help me?"

Of course he will.

The mark will abandon his planned trip and instead accompany her on an endless journey across the country and back as she sells herbal medicines. He will see ninjas always around him, and she will tell him that if he ever leaves her, they will seek to kill him. She will teach him the arts of ninja stealth and passive observation so that he may better protect her—and himself. Over time he will come to forget his old life, and she will trust him with more and more of her secrets. One night, in Baltimore, she will show him what she has never shown any outsider: how to summon a giant toad. "Now we must always be together," she will say. The toad will watch them as they make love.

The next morning neither she nor the toad will be there. The mark will worry, but he will not worry that he has somehow been

32. I trust the terrible meaning of this omen is obvious; if no, please re-consult "Omens v. Portents," p. 32.

conned. He will worry that he has somehow failed her. After lunch, she will return to the room in tears. She will apologize and explain that it was all a con.

She was never being chased by ninjas, she will say, but instead had been ordered by her ninja village to seduce him with her tale and rob him of all his money. But what she did not count on was that she would fall in love. For though he has never received any training in the martial arts or in the use of the climbing hook or the throwing star, she saw from the start that he was, at heart, a ninja.

But now the game was over. In a moment of weakness, she had shown him the Secret of the Toad. This morning she saw her *jyuunin*, the high ninja, who reminded her of her solemn duty. "I must now not only take your money, darling," she will say, "but also your life."

"I do not care for money or life," the mark will say, naturally. "I only wish to be with you."

The woman ninja will relax her killing stance. If that is so, she will say, there is but one option: for him to renounce the outside world and join her ninja village. He must himself become a thief and assassin. But how could she ask him to become a killer, when all he has desired was to save her?

At this point the mark will explain that she need not cry. Throughout this long journey, he too has realized that, in his heart, he is already a ninja. And perhaps thinking both of the love they have shared as well as the power to summon giant animals that will soon be his, he will agree to undergo the long training, the terrible trials, and join her in the shadows forever.

Years ago, as she watched her parents die at the hands of a demon, the ninja vowed never to cry again, but to save every drop of her life and will and forge it into a blade of vengeance. But now she will be unable to contain her tears of happiness. "We shall never be parted, my darling," she will exclaim, kissing his face over and over. She will stare into his eyes adoringly. "Now," she will say, "there is the small matter of the hundred-thousand-dollar initiation fee."

PART SIX

OUR 51 UNITED STATES

LYCANTHROPIC TRANSFORMATION TIMETABLES			
SIXTH SEVENTH			
	MINUTES AFTER MOONRISE/MOONSET		
	to-Wolf	to-Man	Transformation
Werewolf (North American)	10'23"	12'24"	fur receding
Hombre Lobo	9'43"	8'24"	cringing, doubting
Werewolf (British)	8'00"	39'41"	toothy, but self-recriminating
Loup-Garou	8'02"	22'23"	likely to blame self
Varcolac	7'14"	20'13"	wound-licking
Libahunt	7'44"	19'28"	denial
Werebears and Skinwalkers	24'58"	24'32"	blood hibernation

CHARM POTENCY	
silver items	effective
wolfsbane	highly effective
fur girdle removal	moderate
taming love of pure woman	at its peak

ACTIVE

THE STATES, THEIR NICKNAMES AND MOTTOES,
AND OTHER FACTS CRITICAL TO SAFE TRAVEL

As many have forgotten, our nation is divided into states, numbering 51 (of which only 50 are commonly known[33]). They are a remarkable natural occurrence of mysterious origin which when you fit them all together, perfectly cover the continental mass we call the U.S.A., leaving only the small hole or "district" of Columbia, where compasses spin wildly and magnets fail to function. In addition, the U.S. owns several territories and island protectorates, and twenty-five secret space colonies. That is all I can tell you about the space colonies. But if you are surprised to learn that there are secret space colonies, then you are more foolish than I thought.

When I was a child in Brookline, Massachusetts, everyone knew that "Massachusetts" was the "Bay State" due to its enormous bay-leaf-drying industry. And it was often on a eucalyptus-scented evening that I would dreamily ponder the exotic pictures conjured by the nicknames of other states: Rhode Island, or "Li'l Rhodie"; Connecticut, or "Normal-Size Rhodie"; Alaska, or the "Land of Mustaches." Perhaps I was just woozy from the bay leaves, but the nation seemed a magical place then, and I always had very clear nasal passages.

Few children are taught now to recite all the state nicknames and their mottoes, and so I provide this handy and most basic guide to the great jigsaw puzzle that is our nation and its many giant pieces, made of land.

Alabama

NICKNAME: State of the Golden Heads

MOTTO: "We Dare to Sculpt Our Own Heads."

NOTES: In this state, the governor is paid in gold ingots. It is customary at the end of his/her term to melt some number of them and return them to the state as a bust of his/her head. Traditionally, the

---

33. Please see "A Note on Ar," p. 165.

gold sculpting was done by the governor himself. Anti–child labor Gov. William D. Jelks was a particularly nimble sculptor, while George Wallace, for reasons unknown, gave himself a third eye in the middle of his forehead during his last term of office. Now the task is largely given over to professional sculptors and paid consultants, many from out of state, making this, for most Alabamans, a hollow exercise in professional politicking.

Alaska

NICKNAME: Land of Mustaches

SIZE: At 656,424 square miles, it is the largest state. If superimposed on the "Lower 49," it would stretch from Minnesota to Texas, destroying all beneath it.

NOTES: Also known as Seward's Folly or Seward's Icebox after William Seward, who purchased the territory from the Russians in 1867 for the purpose of freezing American presidents. Seward, who was stabbed the same night as Lincoln was shot, believed that had Lincoln reached a massive, frozen tundra soon enough, he might not have died and instead might have been preserved until such time as future science could revive him. Alaska, thus, was designed as an icy safeguard against future assassinations, though it was never used. It is true that Gerald Ford was flown there after Squeaky Fromme's assassination attempt, but instead of being frozen, he visited a hospital and met Eskimos.

Arizona

NICKNAMES: The Complimentary Bolo Tie State, The Arrid Extra Dry State

STATE CAPITAL: Phoenix, which is ritually burned and rebuilt every fourteen years.

NOTES: The state mammal is the ringtail cat, a small, delicate member of the raccoon family known for its keen eyes, opposable thumbs, and consequent lockpicking skills. Since Arizona achieved statehood in 1912, a ringtail has always held an honorary position in state government, enjoying free passage anywhere within the state capitol building in Phoenix. By strange coincidence, the ringtail is always named John McCain. When the actual John McCain refused to be photographed eating chili with the ringtail McCain at Old Smoky's Restaurant in the town of Williams—a long tradition among Arizona politicians—he was accused of having a temper problem and a bad, anti-ringtail attitude.

Arkansas

NICKNAME: The Bauxite State

MOTTO: "In Bauxite, the Future."

NOTES: Arkansas was formed after the Louisiana Purchase by a scientific method using samples of the state of Kansas and the state of Ar^{34}—the latter providing the seed of the state's bauxite veins, the magical ore that is transformed into aluminum, the metal of the future. Many Americans also flock to the continent's only public diamond field, and only a small number of the diamonds found are used to build city-destroying lasers.

California

CURRENT NICKNAME: The Golden State

OLD NICKNAME: Mexico

MOTTO: "Do Not Fear Our Giant Prehistoric Trees."

NOTES: Along with Texas, California was briefly an independent republic, declaring its independence from Mexico in 1846 as "The Bear Flag Republic." After a mere two weeks of self-rule, however, the Bears were defeated in battle and convinced to sign a treaty. They agreed to become citizens of the United States, to stop wearing clothes, and to cut back on the mauling. But the flag remains, still confusing schoolchildren today, who naturally associate California less with bears than with its fine organic produce, borax mining, and giant drive-thru trees.

---

34. Common appellation. Officially known as "Hohoq"—please see individual state entry on p. 164.

Colorado

NICKNAME: The Dwarrodelf

STATE FLOWER: Formerly the Rocky Mountain Columbine, now renamed the Rocky Mountain Pretty, Pretty Flower.

NOTES: Organized as a territory in 1861 by hardscrabble settlers who had come west in search of good skiing and a place to hide their missile defense nerve center. They chose the Rocky Mountains because they were strong and largely Balrog-free, and there they delved deeply, hollowing the earth's heart of gold and building great halls and underground cities. The chief of these was NORAD, a sprawling dark metropolis that was ruled by a talking computer. Some say a few Coloradans still lurk there, in the hard hills, where they stare down from their empty vaults and echoing antechambers in a lonely vigil. But rumors that they will regularly sneak into your hot tub and drown there are largely inventions of the hot tub–grate industry.

Connecticut

CURRENT NICKNAME: The McCormick Brand Nutmeg State

OLD NICKNAME: The All Brands of Nutmeg State

MOTTO: *"Veritas"*

NOTES: The cradle of Yankee ingenuity in the eighteenth and nineteenth centuries, Connecticut gave the nation the cotton gin, the steel fishhook, the first American cigar, the mechanical nutmeg, and the collapsible hog, as well as the first American submarine. The *Turtle*—a one-man, hand-powered submersible used in the Revolutionary War—was the creation of inventor David Bushnell, a citizen of Saybrook and graduate of Yale College, America's most prestigious school of literary theory and Secret World Government.[35] While the *Turtle* failed in its mission to sink the HMS *Eagle*, Yale remains a naval power. From its secret harbor in the New Haven fjord, Yale still sends out one-man submarines to conduct surveillance and to convey secret messages to its branches in Paris, Beijing, and the Hague.

---

35. Please see "Secrets of Yale University," p. 143.

Delaware

NICKNAMES: The Silverstone State, New Sweden

MOTTO: "First in the Union, First in Silverstone!"

NOTES: The fortunes of the "First State" have long been synonymous with DuPont, founded there as a gunpowder and dynamite company in the nineteenth century and now one of the world's largest corporations. Much of Delaware is parkland, an enormous estate owned by the rogue DuPont siblings: Cleve, Reynaud, Doc, Manfred, and Melissa. Long disassociated with the company that bears their name, their mutual loathing makes Delaware the playground of their rivalries. They fight one another endlessly, making frequent use of dynamite, assassins, and teams of lions. Melissa, the youngest, is now in her nineties. No one has seen the eldest, Cleve, since the 1970s, though an annual message is often sent from his lands to the local newspaper wishing health to Delawarians and death to his siblings. Reynaud is said to have extended his life via marvelous chemicals devised by his captive brother, Doc, and to travel the state in a suit of resilient, nonstick armor. Worst of all is Manfred, who lords over Dover, that sad port that accepts the country's military dead, whom, it is whispered, are reanimated by Manfred and employed as his footmen. This is why the press is no longer allowed to photograph the flag-draped coffins. While the DuPont corporation denies the existence of the terrible siblings, its board of directors, like the rest of the state, awaits the champion who will finally end their reign of terror.

Florida

NICKNAMES: The Magic Kingdom, The Battleground State

MOTTO: "3,000 Theme Parks By the Year 3000."

NOTES: When they have neared the end of their productive life, here is where the honored elders of our nation are sent to tend to the magic orange groves. Younger visitors delight at the fascinating antics of the aged, especially after they have been rejuvenated by glowing alien pods. And thousands gather each year to watch the old ones sing and break dance at the Launching of the Harvest, when millions of pounds of citrus are loaded onto sea barges and then towed by manatees up the coast.

Georgia

NICKNAME: "Where Every Street Is Named Peachtree"
STATE COCKTAIL: The "Georgia-on-My-Mind": equal parts Coke, Peachtree schnapps, and dry sherry
NOTES: Georgia is a bounteous state marked by the near supernatural production of two remarkably versatile crops: peanuts and peaches. The former is commonly transformed into peanut butter, various roofing materials, and allergens; the latter are used to make Peaches 'n' Cream Lifesavers, accounting software, and glue. Both are made into schnapps. Martin Luther King, Jr., was born in Atlanta, yet it would take a thousand clones of that great activist for peace and tolerance to erase Georgia's dark reputation as the birthplace of Stalin. Unfortunately, though, conservative anticloning ideologues within the U.S. government have conspired to keep MLK models #1–1000 in stasis in the basement of Georgia State University. Their fate is uncertain.

Hawaii

NICKNAME: The Lost Continent That Is Not Atlantis
MOTTO: *"Ua Mau Ke Ea O Ka Aina I Ka Pono"* ("The Land Mu Is Perpetuated in Righteousness.")
NOTES: The Kingdom of Hawai'i consists of only the tops of the highest mountaintops of what was once the ancient lost continent known as Mu. According to legend, Mu was an advanced, peaceful empire of hovercars and glowing pyramids in which all children were trained as both warriors and poets, largely using an early version of books-on-tape. But their science could not hold back a vengeful sea, and so the empire was swallowed by the waves some fifteen thousand years ago or more. Chaos reigned among the various chieftains who ruled the remaining islands after the continent's demise. It was not until 1810 (A.D. 27,981, Year of Mu) that the islands would be unified

under King Kamehameha the Great, who established a sophisticated constitutional monarchy guided by reason and modeled after the post-Enlightenment European states. Once again, hovercars traveled from island to island. The ukulele was invented, and the king initiated a massive project to raise the Lost Continent using giant balloons and crude nuclear explosives. This proved too threatening to the American-born plantation owners. Under the leadership of the attorney Sanford Dole, and with the backing of the U.S. Marines, they forced the last king to sign a new constitution at gunpoint, which would strip the native Hawaiians of their voting rights, effectively end the monarchy, and halt the ascent of Mu (at about the halfway mark). But: we got another state out of it.

Hohoq (also known as Ar)

NICKNAMES: The Vanishing State, The Ford Thunderbird State

MOTTO: "Please Do Not Seek Us."

NOTES: A large, cloud-encircled plateau that moves mysteriously from place to place throughout America, and frequently goes completely unobserved for decades. Often forgotten on most maps and openly disdained by scientists who have not yet been able to explain it, it is supposedly home to the Thunderbirds—airplane-sized eagles capable of shooting lightning from their eyes, which were once considered a Native American legend. In 2001, when Ford Motor Company reintroduced its Thunderbird model, an attempt was made to capitalize on the legend of the 51st State. As a publicity stunt, 250 Thunderbird cars were sent out to find it and climb the cliffs to their airy heights. Most of the cars were never recovered (none of the drivers ever were). In 2005, one empty vehicle mysteriously washed ashore on Revere Beach in Boston, while another was found near Sacramento, appearing to have been dropped from a great height.

A NOTE ON AR

Hohoq, still known popularly as "Ar," frequently moves across the continent by unknown means and seems to disappear altogether. Early settlers of the American West claimed that it was usually seen after a thunderstorm: a sheer wall of mottled, sandy bauxite in the distance, surrounded by the lacy clouds and bursts of white sunlight that follow a heavy rain.

Some claimed to have seen distant figures atop the plateau, though there was some disagreement over whether they were men or large birds. In any case, the figures seemed indifferent to those enterprising souls below who carved bauxite from Ar's sides (some of which would be used to form Arkansas in 1836). Those who tried to scale the plateau, however, would quickly fall asleep. When they awoke, Ar would be gone.

The first American to walk on Ar (voluntarily) was the anthropologist Franz Boas, who landed his solo zeppelin there as he traveled through British Columbia in 1897.

Boas reported in his diaries that the plateau was inhabited predominantly by aboriginal Americans. As well, he wrote, a minority of German-American families had resettled there throughout the 1850s due to kidnapping by Thunderbirds. The Thunderbird, as you know, is a gigantic raptor, which carries storm clouds in its wings and has a yen for oompah music and smoked meats.

Boas stayed with the natives of Ar as the plateau traveled over the Nechako Range. "As the Thunderbird can take human form," he wrote in a letter to the American Museum of Natural History, which had sponsored his journey, "it is difficult to tell who here is human and who is bird. Both natives and Thunderbirds have been equally kind to me, and

Continued on next page.

both are strangely aloof." The Germans, however, seemed to be simply Germans.

Boas departed the plateau at Bella Cooda after a nightlong potlatch in which he was given many ceremonial masks and smoked sausages that are now on display at the Museum's Pacific Peoples Room. The next morning, a Thunderbird carried Boas in his claws, back to the unmoving lands of North America.

Ar moves without care throughout the United States and Canada. But it became a U.S. state in 1912 after a decade of lobbying by one Meister Schulze.

Schulze was an elderly Aric-Germanic wanderer and artifact peddler who had arrived in Washington shortly after Boas left on his journey. Gnomish and top-hatted, Shulze was nonetheless charismatic. He quickly became Ar's most famous ambassador—and soon its first senator. (A second senator was appointed by the people of Ar, at least according to Schulze, but this person was never seen.)

Senate historians relate that Schulze accomplished little during his single term. But he gained considerable renown and wealth publishing exciting and entirely fictive adventure novels about Ar, the savages who rode the Thunderbirds, the flesh-eating giants known as Geek-ums, and the brave, pith-helmeted Americans who killed them all. (Of the twelve published, only *Blood Ritual of the Bird-Riders* remains in print.)

Boas tried valiantly to counter this stream of nonsense by writing editorials and by building increasingly detailed dioramas of authentic Aric villages out of pipe cleaners. But Schulze had the ear of the newspapers, and pipe cleaners were seen as old-fashioned. Boas was dismissed in the press as a "simple envier and perhaps a lunatic."

In 1920, however, Boas received a visitor: a young man with yellow eyes in a morning coat. He told Boas they had met

Continued on next page.

before, although Boas did not remember it. The man opened his coat, and Boas saw that it was lined with freshly killed mice. From the inside pocket the man drew a letter from Ar and asked Boas to read it aloud in the senate. Boas agreed.

It was only after long petitioning that the great bauxite doors of the senate chamber were thrown open for Boas. Schulze awaited him. His influence had grown in the government, and by his order the chamber was now kept dimly lit by embers, full of incense and smoke, with strange meats hanging by the fires. Schulze had taken to sitting in the Speaker's chair, and from that perch, surrounded by his flatterers, he grinned and watched Boas find his way into the dark room like a blind man.

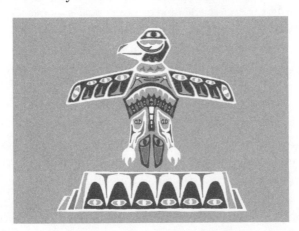

FIGURE 23: *The Great Seal of Hohoq*

The rest we know from the senate minutes: Boas opened the letter. It was on vellum, written in English and German, under the great seal of the plateau, which no one had ever seen before. "'We are Hohoq. We send our greetings to the government of the United States,'" Boas read in a reportedly frail voice, "'and also our apologies.'"

Continued on next page.

The letter went on to explain that the people of the United States had been the victim of an unfortunate deception: They had been greeted by a malicious exile, one who was not duly elected by anyone or anything except his own appetites. "'Schulze, you call him,'" read Boas, "'and he bids you call him 'Master.' But we have our own name for him: Kwakwakala-nooksiwae, the monstrous cannibal-raven. And now it is time to call him home.'"

No one spoke. The fire crackled, and Boas's eyes were watery and unsure. Finally, reported observers, Shulze coughed out a dry, croaking laugh. "Herr Doktor Boas," he said, "we are both Germans and modern men. Western men. Surely you cannot be beguiled by the un-science and myths of the lesser races!"

It was the wrong argument to take with Boas. Boas, who was indeed born in Germany, had rejected his native land's growing anti-Semitism. Here, after all, was the father of cultural relativism, the great historical particularist, who would never dismiss another's false magic merely to burnish his own.

According to the minutes, all nervousness dropped from Boas like a cloak, and outrage glimmered in his eyes. Now, as had been arranged, Boas spoke a few words in another language that were not recorded, as there are no letters to make them.

For only the second time in history, and for very different reasons, the Senate chamber filled with lightning and horrible noise. Great sheets of rain fell from the ceiling, hissing out the fires and washing away Schulze's human disguise, leaving only an enormous bird, black and ragged-winged and choked with rain. In panic, the raven flew blindly and violently into the walls and corners of the chamber, until it was rescued from itself by the talons of another great bird. From the gallery where it had hid, a Thunderbird whom Boas now remembered, with the suddenness of a gasp, as the very Thunderbird who bore

Continued on next page.

him down from the plateau, had shed its black morning coat
and emerged from the dark. Its wings stretched from one end of
the room to the other, and it flapped them twice, casting wind
and rain upon Boas's cheeks as he looked up at it. The Thunderbird caught the raven, now bloodied and slow, in its talons.
And despite its great size, the Thunderbird somehow swept out
of the bauxite doors, taking the former senator–turned-raven
with it, the prisoner weeping in hate and gratitude.

Ar remains a state, though it prefers to be called by the
name it chose for itself, "Hohoq," which is Kwakiutl for "Thunderbird." And it has never sent another representative to Congress. The Thunderbirds do offer a yearly tribute of bauxite to
the government as continued reparation for the shame Schulze
brought upon them. Otherwise the Thunderbirds remain self-
governing and remote as always, and they pay no federal
taxes. As a result, you can get excellent deals on mail-order
cigarettes from them if you can find the secret Web site.

Franz Boas, meanwhile, enjoyed the restoration of his reputation, though he lamented never visiting Hohoq again.

Its last four observed locations were . . .

October 19, 2002—North of Alamosa, California
June 3, 1998—on the West Side of Manhattan
May 21, 1993—near Fargo, North Dakota
February 22, 1984—outside of Winnipeg, Manitoba

Idaho

NICKNAME: The Land of Land and Also Dirt

MOTTO: *"Ore-Ida Perpetua."* (Ore-Ida Forever.)

NOTES: An effort to join with Oregon in 1914 to form the super-state of Ore-Ida was foiled after a brief skirmish with the federal government. Ore-Ida's potato cannons and potato–battery-powered flying machines were no match for the National Guard's metal bullets. Metal bullets have been the norm in Idaho ever since. Also of note is Craters of the Moon National Monument. These stark lava fields provided the backdrop for both the fake NASA moon landing and the fake Mars landing (1923 and 1978, respectively).

Illinois

NICKNAMES: Land of Wormholes, Land of Lincoln Navigators

MOTTO: "State Sovereignty, National Unity, Complete Global Domination Through Wormholes."

NOTES: Illinois's complex system of rivers, canals, underground tunnels, and elevated shipping aqueducts connects the Mississippi to the St. Lawrence Seaway, offering the traveler two distinct ways to sail to Europe. This effect proved so startling at first that many turn-of-the-century newspapers claimed that an amazing interdimensional portal had been discovered—a vast, though exceedingly slow, "wormhole." The name stuck, but the truth is that Illinois contains no more wormholes than most average states. Also note that in literature and the popular imagination, Illinois is said to be home to the fictional city of "Chicago."[36]

CHICAGO? YOU ASK. READ ON . . .

---

36. Please see "Four Dubious Fables of Chicago" on the next page.

FOUR DUBIOUS FABLES OF CHICAGO

I live in New York City, yet I am surprised almost every day by the number of people here who want to talk about Chicago all the time.

These people tell me that they once passed near or through Chicago, and some claim to be *living* there, even as we speak. This is strange enough. But what really surprises me is how many of these self-appointed Chicago experts seem to believe that Chicago actually exists. Not as an idea or as an allegory. They really believe that the city stands there, in all its legendary green-rivered, fire-prone glory, and that once every 100 years, when it rises out of Lake Michigan, you can visit it.

Now, I understand why the concept of Chicago is so alluring. It has been sung to us, like a lullaby, by our culture in story and song for nearly as long as there has been an Illinois.

Most of the novels of Charles Dickens were set in a fictional Chicago so vividly realized that it truly did seem real. Who can forget Fagin's immortal line from *Oliver Twist* when instructing that eponymous orphan on the pickpocket's code: "They pull a knife," said Fagin, "you pull a gun. He sends one of yours to the hospital. You send one of his to the morgue. That's the Chicago Way."

For many years, Hugh Hefner presented Chicago as his snowy, rainy pleasure dome, before revealing his true location in Los Angeles, living in a hyperbaric tube. And most recently the musical *Chicago* was adapted to great acclaim for the screen under the title *Uncle Buck*.

Undoubtedly there is something in us that *needs* Chicago as an idea: a dream as fanciful as the notion of an elevated train. But when you attempt to bring the train to ground, to put it

Continued on next page.

on a map and say *this exists*, it is not merely insane, it threatens to make what is magical merely banal.

So perhaps it would be wise at this point to review what we know about Chicago. The fables, of course, are numerous and varied . . .

1. Depending on whom you believe, Chicago first appeared to either American soldiers stationed at Fort Dearborn, or a Haitian fur trapper named Jean-Baptiste Point du Sable. It was 1772 when Du Sable supposedly saw the city rise out of the lake, named it Eschikagou, and founded a fur-trading settlement there, right in the shadow of the Sears Tower.

2. In 1892, word spread of a fantastic "Columbian Exposition," to be held in Chicago, a glowing white city-within-a-city built in anticipation of the glorious twentieth century to come: a carefree future of civic corruption, gang rule, and innovative public housing. Twenty-seven million people, a quarter of the population of America, left their homes to visit the exposition. They were never heard from again.

Still, the exposition provoked so much heated discussion that *New York Sun* editor Charles Dana legendarily dubbed Chicago "The Windy City." This is, of course, a misremembering of Dana's original wording, which was "Blow Town." But in fact the *New York Sun* did not even start publishing until 2002, and one now wonders if Mr. Dana even existed.

3. Then, in 1900, it is said that the Chicago River actually reversed direction. Some accounts say that this was followed by a hailstorm of snakes and that the river turned bloodred in honor of St. Patrick. In any case, I say: creepy and improbable.

(Which, by the way, will be the title of my new reality tele-

Continued on next page.

vision program about human oddities and unusual stunts, each week featuring clips of me having dinner with a man sporting a beard of bees: *Creepy and Improbable*.)

4. The poet and explorer Carl Sandburg asserted in his poem "Chicago" that the city was populated by half-naked, white-toothed, magnetic dog-men who had enormous shoulders. At first it was believed that Sandburg was merely a dope fiend. Later, it would be learned that he was in fact speaking of Omaha. Also, he didn't exist either.

Time and again, the Chicago-is-real theory simply does not stand up to scrutiny. There are no man-eating vines on the wall of Wrigley Field. No Al Capone. No John Wayne Gacy. These are stories invented to frighten children.

This is not to say that there are not *Chicagoans*. But I would suggest that they are a nomadic people, whose lost home exists only in their minds, and in the glowing crystal memory cells they all carry in the palms of their hands: a great idea of a second city, lit with life and love, reasonable drink prices at cool bars, and, of course, blocks and blocks of bright and devastating fire.

Indiana

NICKNAME: The Unified City and County Government State

MOTTO: "Up-Good Unigov!"

NOTES: In 1970, faced with the difficulty of governing a growing Indianapolis metro area incorporating many distinct townships, an experiment in fused city/county government was launched called Unigov. The Unigov Common Council seamlessly organized the combined civic services of the region and streamlined resource management and foodcake distribution. Local mayors were invited to become Special Ministers of Unigov called "Hoosiers." Those who agreed got to wear beige jumpsuits. Those who refused were allowed to live in peace in Kentucky—or so reported the mimeographed *UnigovMemo*, which replaced all newspapers. In reality, those who refused were sent to the Indiana Dunes to die. But true political power in Speedway One, as Indianapolis was rechristened, rested in UltraGov, the elite clique of tanned, muscular academics that rose to power in 1978. Unlike their beige-jumpsuited underlings, the UltraGov wore orange jumpsuits with yellow piping. Flexing their well-developed triceps and performing feats of telekinesis on television, they declared themselves "the final evolution and perfect expression of centuries of municipal government." While the twelve members of UltraGov were brilliant and extremely attractive, they were unable, finally, to submit their egos to SingleVision, and ended up murdering one another in their Monument Circle BioSphere.

Iowa

NICKNAME: The Hobo State

MOTTO: "Here We Cease Our Motion."

NOTES: The fertile Iowan prairies attracted diverse settlers through the nineteenth century, probably due to the aforementioned fertility and Iowa's traditionally lax regulation of the home appliance industry.[37] One such group was the hoboes. In 1900, Grand Head Pipe Charles Noe founded the National Hobo Convention, which met annually in Britt, Iowa, each August. As to why Iowa would tolerate hoboes in such great numbers, we may speculate that the hoboes paid off the local government in lint goods and clay-baked chickens. More of a mystery is why the hoboes would care to stop moving and gather together in the first place. In 1989, a *Des Moines Register* reporter may have solved the mystery. Examining the long-abandoned convention grounds, he discovered that it was, in fact, nothing but a tarp covered up with stolen sod and garbage. Beneath it a great cavern had been dug. It was clearly the work of hundreds of filthy hands, laboring

---

37. Please see the Panasonic Farm section of "Utopias," p. 208.

over many filthy years. Like all hobo works, the caverns are de-ranged, full of dead ends, superfluous cutbacks, and branches that twist and spiral back on themselves. Most speculate that the "Hobo Hole," as it is now called, was either an attempt to burrow through the globe itself, or was rather a soil mine from which the hoboes drew fuel for the great dirt rocket that took them off this earth in the 1940s.[38]

Kansas

NICKNAMES: The Center, Gateway to Oz

MOTTO: *"Ad Astra Per Meadowlark."* ("To the Stars, Via Meadowlark.")

NOTES: The geographic center of North America is historically located in Osborne County, Kansas. It is said that all armies will bow before the one who controls it. When Bob Dole attempted to seize The Center as part of his 1996 bid to become U.S. president and North American viceroy, The Center's immense power withered his arm and his reason, nearly destroying him. He was saved only by the miracle drug Viagra. Still coveted by both U.S. political factions, The Center is now held in a secret location, somewhere in Kansas, protected by cyclones.

Kentucky

NICKNAME: Land of Sad Grasses

MOTTO: "Fighting Never Proved Anything, Except Who's Better."

NOTES: Bourbon, that great quaff of Kentucky, was originally considered fit only for feeding to horses, and indeed when it was consumed straight out of the bourbon mines it was unpalatable to most non-equines. What we now call the "mint julep" descends from the "speed julep"—a combination of horse bourbon, mint, the native luminous bluegrass, tobacco, and coca leaf—that was fed to racing colts as a

---

38. Please see "Brief Lives of Some Notable Hoboes," p. 102.

pep tonic well before the first Kentucky Derby. It was not until the alchemist Elijah Craig perfected his aging process (allowing the raw spirit to rest for two or more years in a new charred white oak barrel that contained the body of a Kentucky colonel) that the fine, complex, colonel-y liquor that humans enjoy today was first poured.

FIGURE 24: *Only the Bourbon Cask on the Left Contains the Body of a Real Kentucky Colonel*

Louisiana

NICKNAMES: The Emeril State, The State of Intoxication

MOTTO: "Bam!"

NOTES: New Orleans was the first city to offer indoor absinthe faucets, and indeed has always played a cosmopolitan and libertine ragtime beneath America's generally dull Sousa march of rural piety. Outrage rightly grew over the series of "Girls Gone Wild" daguerreotypes that was produced in the "Large Easy" in the 1840s, but there was little that could be done to stop their circulation. For while the state had been purchased by the U.S. as part of the Louisiana Purchase of 1802, the city itself was, for obscure reasons, placed in escrow, where it remains today, technically under the jurisdiction of Gibraltar. This peculiar legal status makes the city a haven for vampires, video-poker enthusiasts, and sub–sea level drinkers of all ages.

Maine

NICKNAMES: Vacationland (for Massachusetts),
The Little Wooden Statue of a Crusty Sailor State
MOTTO: "Remember the Maine!"
NOTES: "The Florida of Canada," Maine has been a haven for lovers of sharp, gravely beaches and painful oceans since nearly its inception in 1622, when it was called "Vacationland." Originally part of Massachusetts, it was kept secret from the rest of the nation by the great Boston families, who wished no intrusion on the vast private retreats and moose experimentation stations they had constructed there. They were finally forced to reveal Maine to the young nation in 1820, when a new free state was required to balance the admittance of pro-slavery Missouri—the so-called Missouri Compromise. Maine residents were informed of their statehood in 1940.

Maryland

NICKNAME: The Peace-Through-Invisible-Lines State
MOTTO: "Manly Deeds, Womanly Hands."
NOTES: The Mason-Dixon line was surveyed and drawn in 1763–1767, ostensibly to establish the border separating Pennsylvania and Maryland. While the border did put a final end to the bloody Penn–Calvert Wars, the true aim of Charles Mason and Jeremiah Dixon was to map the powerful, preexisting "ley line," resonating with earth energy that naturally divided the continent and could be monitored by the British government. Mason and Dixon grew tired and cranky, however, and ceased after about 244 miles. Yet they left along their path many "crownstone" markers that still occasionally hum with powerful druidic magic and still keep watch. It is said that if you whisper the right words to the stones, they will tell you the names of every soul who has crossed the line. This will take the rest of your life.

Massachusetts

NICKNAMES: The Old Bay Leaf Colony, The Fleet Center

MOTTO: *"Ense Petit Placidam Sub Libertate Quietem."* ("By the Sword We Seek Peace, But Peace Only Under Liberty, and Liberty Only Under Justice, and Justice Only Under Victory, and Then Only As a Last Resort, When All Other Options Have Been Exhausted.")

NOTES: Established in 1620 by Liberals, Massachusetts is not actually a state but one of four "Commonwealths," the others being Kentucky, Virginia, and Pennsylvania. U.S. currency is not accepted in these places, so the tourist should change her money for scallops (pronounced, in the amusing Boston accent, "SCAH-lop-sssssssssssss"), horseshoes, hams, and "Pennsy Pennies" (which are also, curiously, scallops), respectively. Through the historic town of Boston (pronounced "Shawmut") winds a painted red line called the "Freedom Trail" that leads visitors past historic sights such as Paul Revere's home, Faneuil Hall, the site of the Boston Massacre, the preserved corpse of Crispus Attucks, the *Cheers* bar, and then straight on to Moscow. It was amusing to have Massachusetts as part of our country, but now, of course, like so much of the coastal nation, it no longer qualifies as America.

Michigan

NICKNAMES: Land of 1,000 Peninsulas, The Auto Zone

MOTTO: "If You Seek a Pleasant Peninsula, and Are Not Satisfied With Florida or Cape Cod, Look Around You: You May Be in Michigan."

NOTES: Most of this state's many peninsulas were purposefully destroyed in the 1980s to create the recognizable "mitten-and-sort-of–a-handlebar" shape in order to court tourists and wolverines, the state mammal. Much to Michigan's embarrassment, there are actually very few wolverines in the state. They once were used to power the great automotive assembly lines of Detroit and to fight the giant worms in that city's subterranean salt mines. Perhaps due to all this strenuous activity, most of the wolverines died off or relocated to Canada. The last was spotted in 1994. It was driving a foreign car.

Minnesota

NICKNAME: Land of a Perverse Number of Lakes

MOTTO: "Minnesota Nice."

NOTES: Minnesota's many, many lakes, some of them so deep as to technically be called "water-pits," were formed naturally and not, as many believe, by the gargantuan footfalls of the giant Paul Bunyan.[39] These lakes are the source of most of the nation's wild rice, public radio, and native lake monsters. "Chessie," the great sea beast of Chesapeake Bay, for example, was initially spawned in Lake Minnetonka, as was Bellagiessie, the canal monster at the Bellagio Hotel, who is an exact replica of Venice's Grandie.

Mississippi

NICKNAME: Old Man River, That Old Man River, He Must Know Something, But Don't Say Nothing

MOTTO: "I'm Tired of Living and Scared of Dying!"

NOTES: The tortured, twisting left-hand border of this state is actually a river called "The Mississippi." It is a large and powerful river, known to swell its banks and completely submerge nearby towns. In 1954, during a drought, the water level dropped and revealed what had once been the town of Old Prentiss, which had been swallowed by the river in 1865. Visitors came from miles inland to walk, awestruck, along Prentiss's once-drowned streets and damp houses —perfectly preserved at the exact moment they were cleansed of life with muddy water. But the river was hungry, and before they knew they had been lured into a trap, the inlanders were consumed by the Mississippi's rushing return. Old Prentiss has not surfaced again, but in recent years, some forty of the sunken towns have been colo-

---

39. Please see "Wisconsin," p. 192.

nized by scuba divers and, under various loopholes in the state law, now thrive as lavish underwater casinos.

Missouri

NICKNAMES: The Show-Me State, The Prove-It State, The Demonstrate-Your-God-Damned-Thesis State

MOTTO: "We Demand That It Be Revealed Immediately."

NOTES: Most experts agree that everything is up-to-date in Kansas City, Mo. With its seven-story skyscrapers, full telephone service, burlesque theaters, and multiple gas buggies, it has gone about as far as it can go. No further progress will be undertaken.

Montana

NICKNAME: Land of Wary Glances

MOTTO: "Holding Back the Sky Since 1864."

NOTES: Through various optical effects, the sky appears bigger here than in most other states, hence its reputation as "frightening sky country." Apart from its sizable Native American population, it is home to nearly ninety-five citizens, 60 percent of whom work the great machines that power the continental divide, pushing eastern rivers to the Atlantic and western rivers to the Pacific, and 40 percent of whom are "Blue Yonder Fighters" who bravely patrol the sky by parachute.

Nebraska

NICKNAME: The Mutual of Omaha Wild Kingdom

MOTTO: "Birthplace of Unicameral Government!"

NOTES: Originally considered part of the arid, infertile "Great American Desert," Nebraska has perfected a style of "scientific farming" that has covered the state with giant cornfields used to feed the giant cows. These massive beasts are constantly being explored for new cuts of steak. In recent years, the Nebraskans have discovered not only the Flatiron Steak, but also the Sizzlebottom Steak and the Double-Cut Cowboy Neckflap Steak.

Nevada

CURRENT NICKNAME: The Funtime Family State for Families!

OLD NICKNAME: The Prostitute State

MOTTO: "The U.S. Government Neither Confirms Nor Denies the Existence of a Nevada State Motto."

NOTES: Nearly 90 percent of the land in Nevada is still owned and controlled by the U.S. government, including that portion known as "Area 51," renowned for its luxurious frozen-alien storage facilities and mile-long buffet. Tourists should note, however, that if you approach the mile-long buffet, you will be shot on sight. Other "Areas" are slightly more accessible: Visitors to Area 52, which houses the frozen head of Bugsy Siegel, can usually evade being shot, while the Black Ops soldiers of Area 48 (which houses captured mole-men) use only bows and arrows. While the lavish resorts of Las Vegas are mostly privately owned, a few concrete, windowless, fluorescent-lit government-owned casinos still exist. By a loophole in the Homestead Act of 1862, anyone who occupies one of the government-owned suites for two years legally owns it.

New Hampshire

NICKNAME: The State Liquor Store State

MOTTO: "Live Free of Motorcycle Helmets and Seat Belts or Die."

NOTES: For centuries, a giant, craggy profile of a man could be seen in the cliffs of Cannon Mountain. Beloved and occasionally worshiped by the citizens of New Hampshire, he was dubbed "The Old Man of the Mountain," and his profile still appears on the reverse of the New Hampshire state quarter. Sadly, in May of 2003, scientists determined that "The Old Man of the Mountain" was not in fact a giant man, but just rocks. The citizens of New Hampshire were so enraged by this betrayal that they tore the face off the mountain with picks. Remaining tourist attractions include: Olde Portsmouthe Towne, Libertarians, and tax-free wine and spirits. However, due to the state's famous civic frugality, visitors are asked to supply their own roads.

New Jersey

NICKNAME: The Too-Easy-to-Mock State

MOTTO: "We Are Defensive About Our Faults."

NOTES: The traveler will note the many attractive service plazas along the New Jersey Turnpike, the most hateful road in America. Each plaza is named for a famous New Jerseyan, and each has its own character: The Thomas Alva Edison Service Plaza is made invisible by the Edison method; the Carvel ice-cream store at the Woodrow Wilson Service Plaza offers an ice-cream cake in the shape of the League of Nations; peyote lovers flock to the truck parking lots of the Allen Ginsberg Service Plaza (and also, coincidentally, the Grover Cleveland Service Plaza, though this site is better known as a favorite of illegitimate children). But be warned that the Ray Liotta Service Plaza is haunted by screaming phantoms, and also only has a Quizno's.

New Mexico

NICKNAME: The Epicenter

MOTTO: *"Crescit Eundo."* ("It Grows Mysteriously Out of the Great Explosion.")

NOTES: Known for its vast supplies of turquoise bracelets and atomic bombs, New Mexico offers the visitor both beauty and disintegration. A rough, dark obelisk currently marks the site of the hypocenter of the first nuclear weapons test at the Alamogordo Bombing and Gunnery Range in 1885. Scientists still do not know exactly how the explosion formed the obelisk. It is either a freak creation of a terrible

FIGURE 25: *Formed by Masonic Ritual?*

force we still do not fully understand, or it is something to do with the Freemasons. As that fraternal order is well known for its obelisk fondness, it is hard to rule them out.[40]

New York

NICKNAME: The Affiliated Businesses of 9/11-Related Tourism State

MOTTO: "9/11 Changed Everything, Even Our Motto, Which Had Been: EXCELSIOR!"

NOTES: "On the morning of September 11, 2001, extremists attacked our way of life by flying two planes into the beloved twin towers of the World Trade Center in lower Manhattan. The extremists also flew a plane into the Pentagon, but that doesn't matter as much, because the Pentagon did not also offer dazzling Broadway plays, world-class shopping, and a Red Lobster in Times Square. So when making your plans to wear an American flag bandana and moon around a mass grave, won't you please consider New York City? Be sure to get your daily '9/11 FunPass,' and ask any citizen for directions to the Ground Zero subway stop. With 3,000 killed that terrible morning, the chances you may be talking to someone who lost a friend or family member to the tragedy are surprisingly good!" (Submitted by the Council of Affiliated Businesses of 9/11-Related Tourism)

North Carolina

NICKNAME: The Anti-Buccaneer State

MOTTO: "First in Flying Pirates."

NOTES: Most now agree that the Wright Brothers' brief flight at Kitty Hawk was probably an optical illusion. But for those twelve magic seconds, North Carolinians held hope that at last they would have some relief from Blackbeard's pirate colonies—founded in the eighteenth century and still the scourge of the Outer Banks in 1903.

---

40. Please see "Washington, D.C.: The City of Magnificent Distances," page 194.

But once the first truly functioning airplane began safely ferrying tobacco and doubloons back and forth over the Barrier Islands, the pirates—always quick learners—quickly adapted the technology to their own terrible purposes. Fashioning crude airfoils out of human skin and sabers, they plundered the new airplanes and terrorized the skies in their rum-powered fighters until well into the twenties, when they were finally wiped out by the war zeppelins.

North Dakota

NICKNAMES: See Below.

MOTTO: "Liberty and Union, Now and Forever, One and Inseparable, Except for South Dakota."

NOTES: Since its secession from South Dakota in 1941, North Dakota has sought a unique identity for itself, largely through the yearly commissioning of random new nicknames, including "The Sioux State," "The Flickertail State," "The Peace Garden State," "The Birthplace of the Macabre," and "The South Dakota of the North."

Ohio

NICKNAME: The Red State

MOTTO: "Baby, You and Me Were Never Meant to Be, But Maybe Think of Me Once in a While."

NOTES: Due to its demographic and economic diversity—from the coal mines of the south to the farms of the west to the light industry and astronaut-growth tubes of the north—Ohio is considered by many to be an important bellwether of political mood. No Republican has ever won the White House without also carrying Ohio, nor will they ever. As of 2004, after a narrow Republican win in the state, the federal government granted Ohio permanent Red State status. If Ohio is truly a microcosm of America, goes the reasoning, then by definition it must be under Republican domination. Hereafter, all of Ohio's twenty Electoral College votes will flow automatically to the Republican nominee in every election, for all time, or until such time as elections are no longer necessary.

Oklahoma

NICKNAME: The Scoured-by-Dust State

MOTTO: "When You Think of Oklahoma, Please Think of the Rousing Song 'Oklahoma!' Do Not Think So Much of the Less-rousing Song 'Trail of Tears'!"

NOTES: In the 1930s, severe dust storms prompted the exodus of a full 15 percent of the state's population: "Okies" who had watched their crops, homes, and sometimes their dogs and cats be devoured by dust before their eyes. Historians differ as to the causes of the "Dust Bowl": some believe the hoboes summoned the storms to show their power as they were aspiring to take over the U.S. government.[41] Others believe the hoboes summoned the storms in order to create more hoboes. In any case, the visitor need not worry any longer about having the skin torn from his bones in seconds by fierce winds of grit and sand: The last dust storm may be viewed in Tulsa, where it is kept, ever-whirling, in the centerpiece tank of that city's world-famous Dustarium.

Oregon

NICKNAME: The Big Beaver Furrier's Dreamland

MOTTO: "In Oregon, Where the Shadows Lie."

NOTES: Prior to the Oregon Treaty of 1846, the Oregon Territory was a rugged land, dangerously overrun with beavers and British settlers, and stretching from the tip of present-day California to the North Pole. Seriously, it was simply gigantic. Parts of Oregon were regularly found in empty lots and basements as far east as Illinois. When Oregon was discovered hanging around the outskirts of Baltimore, President Polk cried out, "Fifty-Four Forty or Fight!" His council of numerologists immediately scryed the meaning: Oregon was to be stopped. After two years of concerted spellweaving and secret bloody battles, the president's geographimancers at last fixed Oregon's northward boundary to the 49th parallel. With Oregon's back to the sea, the government would continue long after Polk's

---

41. Please see "Brief Lives of Some Notable Hoboes," p. 102.

death to push Oregon south from Canada and west from the Rockies to its current boundaries, where it seethes now, perpetually covered in a dark cloud of marijuana smoke, ever dreaming of conquest.

Pennsylvania

NICKNAMES: Keystonia, Perfect Ten-Sylvania

MOTTO: "Like the Sausage Known As 'Scrapple,' It Is Better That You Not Know What Goes Into Pennsylvania, But Instead Enjoy the Fatty, Sagey Whole."

NOTES: While sometimes literally overshadowed by the towering, mysterious chocolate factories of Hershey, Pa., William Penn's empire offers much more to the visitor than merely rumors of secret chocolate rivers tended by murderous dwarves: the churning steel bogs of Pittsburgh; the scrapple fields, coal mines, and Amish training grounds of Central Pa.; and of course, Philadelphia, birthplace of American independence and still the home of its giant-bell-cracking industry.[42]

FAST FACTS ABOUT PHILADELPHIA

—The word "Philadelphia," from the Greek, literally means "Pennsylvania."

—It has the highest number, per capita, of Benjamin Franklin impersonators in the country.

—Someday all of the Benjamin Franklin impersonators will fight all of the Mark Twain impersonators, flooding valleys and destroying whole towns in their wake, until nothing is left.

—Harrison Ford lives here and protects Amish children.

Continued on next page.

---

42. Please see "Fast Facts About Philadelphia" on this page.

—Bryn Mawr College, a small but esteemed school of witch-craft and wizardry in the city's western suburbs, is sometimes visible by day.

—Philadelphia is at the cutting edge of some of today's most exciting new developments in sandwich technology. The sand-wiches here are so large and complex and sublime that they contain whole philosophies. Some have the complete oral tra-ditions of several ancient cultures hidden within the roll alone.

—Philadelphia was one of the thirteen East Coast cities called "home" by Edgar Allan Poe, and it was here that he hosted the first of his many Christmas Literary Extravaganzas. Held in 1839, it was, by contemporary accounts, a grand affair, involv-ing feats of literary memorization and drunken sword canery, and a chorus line of murderous orangutans. Poe was dressed as Santa Claus, but at this point in his career this was hardly unusual. After reciting "Tamerlane," he famously brought out his child bride Virginia and seated her on his lap. "What would you like from Santa this year?" he asked. And she replied, "The modern detective story." And so he invented it then and there, writing "The Murders in the Rue Morgue" using only a checkerboard, a bottle of brandy, and a map of Paris. At this point, the police chased Poe back to Baltimore.

Rhode Island

NICKNAMES: Li'l Rhodie, The Little State That's Full of Absinthe Fiends

MOTTO: "Hum. Ho. Did You Wake Me?"

NOTES: Before becoming the Pepsi One state, Rhode Island was famous for its thirst for "coffee milk," fresh local milk combined with a sugary coffee syrup ("Autocrat" is the favored local brand, though some coffee-milk partisans prefer "Despot" or "Totalitarian") and gently laced with absinthe. The drink was traditionally enjoyed in a mansion, hence the imposing, forty-room "summer cottages" and "syrup shacks" of the robber barons that grew like barnacles upon the Newport shore in the nineteenth century. It is believed that the dreamy melancholy associated with coffee-milk addiction may be the reason Rhode Islanders never attempted expansion beyond their minuscule borders, and it almost certainly is responsible for the novels of Rhode Islander H. P. Lovecraft. Absinthe was finally outlawed in 1992, and Rhode Island slowly awoke from its dark dream.

South Carolina

NICKNAME: Land of Two Mottoes

MOTTO: As noted, South Carolina is one of the few states to have two mottoes, both enshrined on the state seal. The first is *"Animis Opibusque Parati"* ("Prepared in Mind and Resources"); the second is *"Dum Spiro Spero"* ("Hang On. We Are Not Sure About That First Motto").[43]

NOTES: While South Carolina is rightly known for the fascinating self-contained Gullah communities of the Sea Islands, where descendants of West African slaves speak a creole tongue of various African dialects and Colonial-era English, one should not overlook the more recent self-contained golfing communities that have sprung up along the coast. Sheltered behind charming picket fences (some electrified), exists a world out of time: brand-new identical homes shaded by replanted live oaks, and porches that look directly out upon the immaculately tended green (or, if you are less wealthy, upon the brand-new recycling center). Such communities as Oldfield, Palmetto Links, and King Charles Town have managed to protect golf's unique cultural homogeneity, while allowing their residents to live in the peace that comes with knowing that golf is truly "a good walk spoiled . . . by awesome golf!"

---

43. Dum Spiro Spero, by the way, was also the name of the mayor in the long-running South Carolinian comic strip *Li'l Golfie,* which told the wacky adventures of a naïve but honorable country boy growing up in a private golfing community.

South Dakota

NICKNAME: The Original Mount Rushmore State

MOTTO: "Under God and the Stony Gaze of the
Presidents, the People Rule."

NOTES: Natural erosion and dynamite are responsible for the eerie colossal faces that peer out from South Dakota's Black Hills. Most famous of these, of course, is the Mount Rushmore National Memorial in Keystone, featuring the massive visages of Lincoln, Jefferson, Washington, and Roosevelt (the latter sporting the world's largest stone pince-nez). Envy of Rushmore drove North Dakotans to break off from the once-unified state in 1941. Occasionally, bands of North Dakotan raiders still sneak across the border and steal the monument in hope of attracting a few tourists. The scheme is rarely successful, and the monument is usually trucked back to the south within a few weeks.

Tennessee

OLD NICKNAME: The Volunteer State

NEW NICKNAME: The Forced Conscription State

MOTTO: "You'll Meet Honest Men and Pickpockets
Skilled. You'll Find That Bus'ness Never Closes Till
Somebody Gets Killed."

NOTES: Tennessee gave us the blues, via W. C. Handy, country via the Grand Ole Opry, and that strange, swiveling fusion of the two that was programmed into the android that replaced the infant Elvis Presley. But let me answer the question that is really on your mind. To clarify: while similar, and also made from sour mash, "Tennessee Whiskey" is not bourbon at all, but a barroom euphemism for the semen of an intoxicated person after it has been filtered through ten feet of maple charcoal. This naturally will not be confused with the "true whiskeys" of Jack Daniel's and other fine Tennessee distillers, for it is obvious at first taste that these are DELICIOUS WHISKEYS and NOT SEMEN.

Texas

NICKNAMES: The Homeland, More Mexico
MOTTO: "Friendship, Except When Betrayed, or
Approached by Strangers."
NOTES: You have heard the saying that everything is bigger in the
Lone Star state, and it is true that the cats are the size of dogs and the
dogs are the size of European cars. But Texans themselves are of nor-
mal proportions, with normal-sized dreams and loves, who just hap-
pen to own cars that are the size of twenty-five European cars.

Utah

NICKNAMES: The Beehive State, The Hive
MOTTO: "I Love Bees."
NOTES: Utah is not a natural home to the bees; the state's fascination
with the insect stems from the name originally proposed for the
Utah Territory by its first governor, Brigham Young: "Deseret,"
which means "honeybee" in the Book of Mormon. It was meant to
convey industriousness and thrift and to promote a hivelike society
in which every citizen lived in a waxy cell. But the Church of Latter-
day Saints was surrounded by controversy in the mid-nineteenth
century, and many outsiders feared a long-standing rumor that the
Mormons hoped to train an army of killer bees to cleanse the nation
of unbelievers with vicious stinging. It was nonsense of course, but
the territory did have to agree to give up beekeeping in order to join
the Union under the new name of Utah. To this day, visitors are
asked to check their pet bees at special facilities at the border, however, along with their extra wives.

Vermont

NICKNAME: New Connecticut
MOTTO: "YEEAAARRGH!"
NOTES: Many come here expecting to see only hippies living in huts
made of maple syrup. Well, you'll find them. But do not overlook the
state's long and curious history of rugged individualism. It was, after

all, a separate country until 1920. The last president of the Nation of Vermont was drunken, swaggering Ethan Allen IV. He and his cabinet were descendants of the original Green Mountain Boys, the ragtag militia that in 1775 took the mountains back from the British, who had stolen and hidden them in the vaults of Fort Ticonderoga. There is a legend that Allen lives on, and that someday soon he will descend from his Northeast Kingdom and once more give the great, half deranged "YEEAARGH!" that the prophecies tell us will announce his return.

Virginia

NICKNAMES: The Old Dominion State, The Mole Dominion State

MOTTO: *"Sic Temper Molemannis!"* ("Thus Always to Mole-Men!")

NOTES: Though one of the oldest and grandest states, Virginia is not, as it has sometimes claimed to be, *700 years old.* Nor was it anything but a minor province of the Dominion, the surface empire briefly established by the mole-men before the Europeans came and the mole-men returned to the Lands Below. Someday I will tell you about the mole-men and the Seven Gates to the Hollow Earth, but for now you can be assured that none of them are in what we now call Virginia. Still, there remain vestiges of the Old Dominion mole-man charm in Virginia's gracious cities, its gentlemen's habits of feeling one another's faces when meeting, and the mole-man palace known as Monticello.

Washington

NICKNAME: The Olde Boeing State

MOTTO: "We Are a State, Not a District of Columbia."

NOTES: Composed of territory retaken from Oregon, the Dark Land, Washington was initially so named in 1853 in an attempt to divert European tourists from the nation's capital. No one expected a small salmon-packing and -shipping company, then operating under the name of Micro-Soft, to change the face of Washington forever. Over

the next 150 years, Microsoft grew into an international super-cor-
poration providing the nation not only with salmon but also various
white-fleshed fish, frozen-fish entrees, and mechanical salmon. By
the year 2000, 90 percent of all American homes were sold "pre-
loaded" with at least one mechanical salmon. The Seattle area especially prospered during the mecha-salmon boom, and young people
flocked to the progressive "City of Needles." After the European
tourists, this was Washington's second great goatee wave.

West Virginia

NICKNAME: Kanawha

MOTTO: "The Film *Deliverance* Was Shot in South
Carolina, Not West Virginia; Indeed, Our Rate of
Murderous Banjoists Is Well Below That of
Massachusetts."

NOTES: West Virginia was originally called Kanawha—a mole-man
word meaning "Mountain Men Are Always Free"—when it seceded
from Virginia to take the Union side in the Civil War. There is little
flat land here, and the people of West Virginia long ago adapted to
near-vertical living, either by carving mansions into the mountain-
sides or by suspending cities from ropes tied from mountaintop to
mountaintop. Vistors who suffer from vertigo, however, should
probably only visit the deep coal and marble mines.

Wisconsin

NICKNAMES: The Big Man State, The Carnation Coffee-
Mate Non-Dairy Creamer State

MOTTO: "Daughters of Babe and Lucy Sing."

NOTES: Despite claims to his legend from the lumber camps of Minnesota and Michigan, folklorists and giantists generally agree that
Paul Bunyan lived and died in the north woods of Wisconsin. Many
of the feats attributed to him are false: He did not create the Grand
Canyon by dragging an ax behind him or smoke a pipe made of a single giant tree, and his farts are not the source of the San Francisco

Fog. These, and the slander that he fathered and then consumed 1,000 giant children, are likely lies spread by Johnny Appleseed, who, as a Swedenborgian, detested giants. The fact is that Bunyan was only a casual lumberjack and something of a recluse. He always rued the annual "Big Man Conference," when he and his giant colleagues Pecos Bill, John Henry, Jack Magyar, William Huge-Muscles, and Norman Mailer would meet atop a gargantuan rattlesnake to share news and discuss the fine points of raising gigantic livestock. "I do not mind the meal of a million biscuits each, I have to say," Bunyan scratched into his diary, made of a single forty-foot-tall stone slab. "But it is sad to hear Bill whoop and holler, more loudly every year, as if he could shout down the truth the way he used to shout down the West Wind. We myths of old industry and manual labor are finished. Only the retail giants, like Big Box Olaf, that ass, and Starbuck Ikea, will survive."

It is true, however, that the congress of Babe the Blue Ox and Lucy the Purple Cow did produce the first two million of Wisconsin's dairy cattle. And most Wisconsinites still grease their giant skillets by wearing skates made of bacon rinds or, in the Madison area, flaxseed oil.

Wyoming

NICKNAME: The Gold Standard State

MOTTO: "Equal Rights, Equal States."

NOTES: One of only two states that are perfect parallelograms, Wyoming takes its nickname from its early ambition to become the "gold standard" against which all other states would be measured. Upon its admittance in 1890 as the 44th state, it proposed that all new states should be shaped exactly like it, and all prior states should redraw their borders until the United States became "a glorious, self-similar nation of thirty-one states equal in all measures."

WASHINGTON, D.C.:
THE CITY OF MAGNIFICENT DISTANCES

After the initial states were named, our nation's founders were then faced with the question of "The Mysterious Region" or the "District of Haunting Emptiness"—those lands cradled by the Potomac River that belonged to no state at all. Debate raged over whether to make this land into a great federal city, or to honor George Washington's request and give it to his brothers in the international fraternity of Freemasons.

In 1790, it was difficult to say no to George Washington. And so Freemason Pierre L'Enfant was commissioned to design a "City of Magnificent Distances," one that would reflect the gracious symmetry and classical proportions so loved by the Freemasons, and that would interact with the region's strange properties—its streams that travel uphill; its lack of magnetic north; its magnificent natural reflecting pools—to open a portal through which the eternal, floating eye of the Great Architect could shine down on the new country forever.

George Washington, ever modest, wished to name the city after Masonic legend, suggesting either "Solomon-Town" or "Mathemagic Land." But the cult of personality surrounding the first president had already grown strong, and against his wishes, the new city was called Washington, District of Baphomet, and later, Columbia.

At eleven square miles—the powerful "Master Builder" number of classic numerology—the city is composed of a normal grid pattern of numbered and lettered streets that then have diagonal avenues tossed all over them like a bunch of pick-up sticks. But while he was a great fan of pick-up sticks, L'Enfant's plan was hardly random. He wished to give the vis-

Continued on next page.

itor the sense of two cities inhabiting the same temporal space at once, thus reflecting the Masonic obligation to both the mundane and Masonic worlds. A Freemason should be able to navigate Washington easily, even intuitively. An outsider, on the other hand, would become instantly nauseated the moment he stepped within its borders.

It was thanks to the great ballooning craze of the early nineteenth century that the first and broadest outlines of the Masonic symbolism that L'Enfant had traced into the city's streets were observed. But it was not until the advent of spy satellites during the Civil War that the full extent of L'Enfant's urban conjuring could be revealed. . . .

TABLE 16: WASHINGTON, D.C., AS SEEN FROM GREAT HEIGHTS	
At balloon height...	The eye may see an Inverted Pentagram formed by the streets and avenues connecting Dupont Circle, Logan Circle, Scott Circle, Washington Circle, and Mount Vernon Square, and culminating in the final point: the White House. Bisecting the pentagram, 16th Street directly connects the White House to the House of the Temple, the national headquarters of the Scottish Rite of Freemasonry. From this height one can clearly observe the black, windowless horse-drawn carriages that even today are used to carry secret orders to and fro between them.
At double balloon height...	The eye may further discern a Compass, the chief symbol of the Masonic Order, formed by Pennsylvania Avenue and Maryland Avenue, with the Capitol Building as its joint. It is combined, as per tradition, with a Square formed by Louisiana and Washington avenues. Originally the streets were lined with luminous granite so that the Compass and Square would glow when seen from above—though by whom, it is not clear, and the effect is now largely spoiled by electric street lamps.

Continued on next page.

TABLE 16: *continued*	
At zeppelin height...	One may see that the access roads surrounding the Capitol form the image of a rabbit attacking a snake with a trowel while holding a candle. Again, these are common Masonic symbols, the meaning of which should be apparent.
At jet aeroplane height...	The city's 33 Great Pyramids and 33 Honored Sphinxes clearly form the outlines of the fractal we now call the Mandelbrot set.
At spy satellite height...	Another rabbit can be seen, this time attacking the Lamb of Willful Ignorance and also what appear to be some mice.
At Lockheed-Martin Orbital Zeppelin height...	It becomes clear that the land surrounding Washington itself takes the shape of the entire United States, which, it can plainly be seen, is a kind of square with some peninsulas sticking off of it—another important Masonic symbol. At this height, the city of Washington itself resembles a dot, representing the Origin of All Things in the Pupil of the Eye of the Great Architect.

FIGURE 26: *Here Is a Familiar Sight....*

Continued on the next page.

FIGURE 27: *Now Look at the Same City from Space: Can You Spot the Hidden Figure?*

Please also note . . .

The Washington Monument, lying in direct line with the Capitol and the White House, is an Egyptian obelisk built with stones donated from Masonic lodges throughout the world. The monument was first proposed in the 1830s, but it was not completed for another fifty-odd years as the Masons perfected the spells and technology required to launch the monument into space. There, they hoped, George Washington's bones, concealed in the pyramidion, would be reanimated by the radiation of a distant red sun. However, Washington's family refused to relinquish the body of our first president to the Masons, and the plan remains stalled to this very day.

The Washington Metro, the city's eerily clean subway system, was built in 1976 under a deal in which the Freemasons would provide sets for the film *Logan's Run.* If you examine the map

Continued on the next page.

of the train system on its side, the lines draw the face of enter-
tainer and Freemason Telly Savalas.

Uncanny, isn't it?

There are those who claim that all of these images evince an
ambition on the part of Freemasonry to guide the U.S. government toward a New World Order of their own design. This
does not seem to be accurate, however. While there is some
evidence that a small group of rogue Masons may indeed have
once wanted to rule the world, their ambitions were, like most
such groups, quickly checked once Yale University caught
wind of their audacity and dispatched an elite team of Whiffenpoofs to put down the plot.

That said, L'Enfant's design did succeed in its primary goal
of summoning the Great Architect. It was 1814, at the height
of the British-American War. As the British raided Washington under the command of Robert Ross, the sky darkened. "It
was as if a storm approached," wrote Ross afterward, "until it
grew over-dark to be natural, and every colour, in every face
and garment, was paled. Then, with a horrible ease and swift-
ness, heaven split, opened, and looked upon us."

The Eye, it is said, filled the sky, as indifferent and mono-
chromatic as its image on the dollar bill. For some five hours,
it looked here and there upon panicked Washingtonians and
invading Britons alike. During this time, the Eye blinked once
and, at this moment, the earth groaned, and many fell to tears,
and the presidential mansion was instantly consumed by green
flame. After initially attempting to repel the Eye, President
Madison fled to Virginia, swimming the Potomac in his clothing and nearly perishing in its waters, which had been transformed into bile. When the Eye finally closed, Washington
was in fiery ruins. All of this would be blamed on the British in
the official histories, of course. But the real story is more complex, as ever, and the Eye always unfathomable.

PART SEVEN

THERE IS MORE PAST
THAN YOU THOUGHT

LYCANTHROPIC TRANSFORMATION TIMETABLES

SEVENTH SEVENTH

	MINUTES AFTER MOONRISE/MOONSET		
	to-Wolf	to-Man	Transformation
Werewolf (North American)	14'21"	12'24"	casual rudeness
Hombre Lobo	12'32"	10'24"	sore throat
Werewolf (British)	13'43"	43'12"	wet fur smell only
Loup–Garou	29'00"	24'02"	quick to accuse others of lycanthropy
Varcolac	42'12"	21'21"	insomnia, headaches
Libahunt	32'31"	24'29"	laziness, dry-mouth
Werebears and Skinwalkers	voluntary	voluntary	watch out!

CHARM POTENCY

silver items	all items, even spoons, are effective
wolfsbane	out of season
fur girdle removal	best bet
taming love of pure woman	only produces shame

NINE PRESIDENTS WHO HAD HOOKS FOR HANDS

The association of hooks with pirates began with J. M. Barrie, author of *Peter Pan*, whose "Captain Hook" popularized the still-seductive concept of extremely sharp, largely useless seafaring prosthetics. In fact, though, it cannot be proven that any nonfictional pirate ever replaced his hand with a hook.

Most believe that Barrie was simply caught up in the anti-pirate vogue that was sweeping Edwardian London's literary circles, just as he had previously succumbed to the equally irrelevant "Anti-Red-Indian Society" and later would fall in with the anti-Vikings. But some more provocative historians suggest that Barrie's slander of the pirates served a secret purpose: to draw public attention away from the very real, if clandestine, practice of hook-wearing among American presidents.

Not *all* presidents wore hooks, but enough did to suggest, at least to some, a conspiracy. These theorists suggest that the hook was a bloody symbol, a ritual of self-mutilation that displayed the presidents' loyalty and symbolic role as the "severed right hand" of their masters, the secret order of the Illuminati—which just happened to be headquartered in the attic of J. M. Barrie's home. Coincidence?

It's a compelling story, to be sure. But it cannot be ruled out that the hook was merely a fad, or even a functional consideration, as hooks are sharper than fingers. In any case, known hook-handed U.S. presidents include:

— Jefferson (who designed his own hook)

— Van Buren (known as "Old Kinderhook")

— Garfield (when President Garfield was shot,
    Alexander Graham Bell attempted to locate the
    bullet with a crude metal detector of his own

invention; instead, he discovered "a curved, metallic sharpness in the vicinity of the wrist's end."
Historians agree: hook)

—T. Roosevelt (first draft: "speak softly and pierce
their eyes with a golden hook")

JOHN SINGER SARGENT

FIGURE 28: *T.R., an Asthmatic, Used His Hook
(here concealed) to Whittle His Own Inhaler*

—F. Roosevelt (note: his hook was actually a
wheelchair)

—Nixon (many believe that the sight of his horrific
hook lost him the first televised debate with
Kennedy, who was hookless)

—Bush I *and* II (however, Bush II replaced his hook
with a chain saw in an effort to seem less privileged)

—Edward "Thach" Teach, a.k.a. Blackbeard
(although technically, President Blackbeard
was only President of the Pirates)

WERE YOU AWARE OF IT?

You know all the famous myths about our nation's first president:
that he wove his first wig himself from the hairs of the dog he
killed so his family could eat. That he rid our nation of the plague
of cherry trees. That beneath his gloves he had the giant, hairy
paws of a bear. That he was our nation's first president. These
are all charming tales.

But were you aware that George Washington . . .

. . . grew hemp?

. . . distilled his own rye whiskey?

. . . smoked 70 cigars a day?

. . . had a rudimentary crystal meth lab in the basement of
Mount Vernon?

. . . kept a laudanum-soaked wad of cotton in his cheek at all
times?

. . . was turned on to hashish by Sally Fairfax, the wife of his
best friend, whom he would love from afar for the rest of his life?

. . . delivered his farewell address at Fraunces Tavern while
high on Madeira and Red Bull?

. . . ate 25 grains of French ecstasy daily "as a digestive"?

. . . wrote *A Book of Etiquette* at the age of sixteen, including
a final admonition to: "Labor to keep alive in your breast the little
spark of celestial fire called 'cocaine?'"

Continued on next page.

> . . . had false teeth that were not made out of wood but other human teeth?
>
> HOW COULD YOU BE AWARE OF IT IF *THEY* DON'T WANT YOU TO KNOW!!!!??

COLONIAL JOBS INVOLVING EELS

Eels, as any schoolchild knows, were the true main course at the Pilgrims' first Thanksgiving, largely because the eels themselves had eaten all the turkeys.[44] While it's difficult to imagine now, because they are so disgusting and now so rare, eels played a critical role in the economy and culture of colonial New England. Once our nation's rivers were glossy and black with majestic herds of eels, but they proved too tempting as a food source, and many found them to be just too spooky to tolerate. What eels were not eaten were often killed out of sheer angry terror. By the time Benjamin Franklin, that famous turkey-lover, began attacking the eels in a series of vicious aphorisms in his almanacs, they had already largely disappeared from the landscape and recorded history. Only in the contemporary occupations of the period does a reflection remain of this important and conflicted relationship.

PALING MAN: A legitimate eel merchant.

EEL PICKER: A person who sorted through the village trash to find reusable eels.

---

44. Specifically I am discussing *Anguilla rostrata,* and not the moray eel, the electric eel, or its cousin, the sleeping-gas eel, which were not brought to the New World until 1917.

EEL AND BONE MAN: An itinerant merchant of eel carcasses and especially eel teeth. (See *SCRIMSCHONGER,* below.)

EEL CRIER: A young man who was posted to watch at the edge of a town or settlement for eels. Often an unintelligent person.

EELWRIGHT: Maker of false eels as decoys or for decorations. False eels were generally made of river mud. This occupation was the more respectable outgrowth of the esoteric profession known as eel-animism. It wouldn't be until 1777 that the gonads of the eel were discovered by Mondini, proving them to be fish. Even then, many still believed the theory first posited by Aristotle that eels were born of the dank river soil itself. Only the famed eel-animist Mercy Weber ever claimed to have successfully created an eel from mud, but her procedure could not be tested due to her being burned alive, appropriately, as a damnable witch.

RATTER: Someone who caught rats to throw at eels to distract them. It was well known that an eel would stare at a rat for hours, allowing a human a quick escape.

EEL CHECKER: Once the eels were first spotted on land, an eel checker was often employed to check a home for hidden eels and to check under wagons for same. This was not a skilled job and should not be confused with an *EELSMELLER,* who was an artisan trained in the art of detecting eels that had disguised themselves as Dutchmen.

EEL ALMANACKER: Many printed almanacs predicted the eel seasons, those periods when the eels would be plentiful, and when they would disappear for months on end to spawn. An eel almanac would also include a calendar of when the eels would be wistful, secretive, or accusing.

SCRIMSHANDER or SCRIMSCHONGER: An artisan who carved scenes of daily colonial life in delicate, small etchings upon eel teeth. Many family portraits and early images of colonial life were immortalized on eel teeth.

TOOTHSMITH: A dedicated eel-tooth polisher and seller. The best eel teeth were those found lodged in trees, which eels would often attack at night.

EEL METERER: One who wrote poems about eels. When the eels proved amphibious and began walking on land, they became objects of deep and fearful fascination. A traveler would pass one on the road and feel the weight of its muddy eyes watching him. Later the eels took to knocking on doors. It is not clear why they would do this, or how. A woman at home might hear a knock at twilight and look up from where she might be hair-spinning by the hearth and go to the door. After some moments' discerning, she would spy in the dusk two or three (never more than four) eels by the brush. When asked what they wanted, the eels would not respond. You might think the colonists would appreciate their dinner coming to their door. But curiously, most found these visits to be more ominous than appetizing. Some reported that the eels seemed to be peering not at them, but into the house behind them. Were they yearning for the comfort of the fire? Or lamenting the death of their fellows, often burbling in the hearth in a popular eel-and-parsley stew?

Still, even the most eel-dreading of colonists recognized a kinship. Like the colonists themselves, the eels were pilgrims, each year leaving the freshwater lakes to take to the ocean, and there to spawn in secret places in the depths of the Sargasso Sea. The young eels, an inch long and transparent and vulnerable, would then travel thousands of miles, eluding predators, somehow sensing their way back to the brackish waters of the swamps, the slow rivers, and their silty bottoms. There they would lurk and grow and ponder their eternal homelessness as a species.

Fear and strangeness, of course, beget stories, and the poets of the time, ever happy to profit from both, took up the eel as a popular subject. And so many folktales were spawned of Dan Crate, the Brackish Man, who tied eels together to build a rope ladder to the clouds, and at the same time of Sleek Cynthia, the noble eel who stared down the sea.

EEL TONGUER: One who learned the language of the eels.

EEL-ORPHAN: A human child raised by eels after his parents had died or had willfully given him up to become an eel tonguer. The eel tonguer's parents were usually held in high regard for their sacrifice, though one printed memoir by an eel-orphan, *The Eel-Boy's Confession and Spelling Handbook,* suggested that the author was much happier with the eels.

ROD-MAN: Also known as an eelpoker. Self-explanatory.

SIX OATHS OF THE VIRTUOUS CHILD

Poor Richard's Almanack was Benjamin Franklin's most successful commercial endeavor (not counting the United States and the frozen turkey). But few know it was a direct rip-off of his own brother's *Rhode Island Almanac,* which in turn drew inspiration from their common antecedent, *Duncan's North American True Almanack.*

Duncan's would be wholly forgotten now were it not for that volume's "Six Oaths of the Virtuous Child," which was commonly recited in public schoolrooms long before the Pledge of Allegiance was written, and was famously intoned by Eugene Cernan upon the Apollo program's last visit to the moon, at which point, apparently, the astronauts were running out of things to say.

Today shall not be wasted. I shall rise before the sun, so that I may then watch my family as they slumber, with intent waiting eyes.

I shall honor my mother today, and I shall tell Father he is powerful.

Today I shall be clean. I shall not touch my teeth, knowing that the oils of my skin shall cause them to disintegrate. I shall instead hone them with a good steel twice after prayers.

I shall be a faithful child, and I shall ever make science my enemy. Also eels.

At day, I shall perform my chores and duties happily, and if I see an eel, I shall kill it before it may speak to me seductively of its lazy life on lazy river bottoms.

At night, I shall dream of more labor, and in my sleep I shall smile with sharpened teeth, knowing that today has not been wasted.

WERE YOU AWARE OF IT?

The "Federalist Papers" were written by John Jay, Alexander Hamilton, and James Madison. But on the page, and indeed around town, the trio went under the collective name of "Publius."

But did you know that before settling on this famous pseudonym, they first considered . . .

Richard Bachman?

Superblius?

Mad Jaymilton?

Mummenschanz?

DID YOU READ THAT IN ANY OF YOUR HISTORY BOOKS?!!

UTOPIAS

History has shown us the benefits of Utopia. There is not a single problem on earth that could not be solved by gathering a bunch of people in a remote location, dressing them alike, and housing them in cities that are either perfect squares or perfect circles.

The term "Utopia" was, of course, coined by Thomas More, the sixteenth-century English humanist who was later canonized by the Vatican for his remarkable innovations in self-flagellation. More described a crescent-shaped island that was home to an orderly and peaceful nation—collectivist in nature, deeply spiritual, and yet deeply tolerant of its many religions—and dotted by dozens of perfectly square cities.

Readers debated whether More's *Utopia* was intended as a reflection of the world he saw around him or as a vision of the world as he wished it to be. A great number believed it to be an allegorical system for raising rabbits, and indeed many current rabbit farms thrive by what is now known as the Lapine Utopian Method.[45]

But in 1972, the mist-drenched island itself was discovered off the coast of Uruguay, and it became clear that *Utopia* was merely a travelogue. Sadly, the real Utopia is no longer accepting new citizens. But More's discovery inspired many idealistic planned communities here in the United States—Brook Farm and New Harmony being two better-known examples. And a few of those that did not end in bankruptcy, food riots, murder parties, and fire are still open to the curious today.

THE SAW CREEKERS

One of many utopian societies founded during the Great Awakening of the mid-nineteenth century, the Saw Creek colony drew intellectuals from all over the East Coast to the Pocono Mountains to join its experiment in social uniformity and consistent humiliation.

---

45. Please see "How to Raise Rabbits for Food and Fur: The Utopian Method," p. 211.

Since no member was supposed to "fancy himself above God, above nature, and above the group," the Saw Creekers sought to neutralize all natural beauty and charisma by requiring members to wear their trousers very high and cut their hair in the shape of Napoleon's hat.[46] It was one of the few utopian communities to forego agriculture or manufacturing in favor of tourism, and it still prospers today by renting out shitty cabins to vacationers. The pants remain high, but the haircuts have given way to simple obesity.

THE CARLSBAD GUANISTS

As early as 1920, visitors flocked to the newly opened Carlsbad Caverns in New Mexico. They came to marvel at the great underground halls, to listen to the song of the caverns' million Mexican freetail bats, and especially to see the Guanists. The Guanists were a group of about a dozen families who lived by candlelight, gathering bat guano and fashioning it into all sorts of clever devices—fruit peelers, little statues of famous men, perpetual-motion machines, etc. They wore white bedclothes at all times and were prone to colds and guano fever. And yet they were seductive: By all accounts they were touched by an otherworldly grace, with beautiful pale skin and faintly luminous eyes. They would emerge from the deep caves carrying guano candles, singing strange hymns that they said the bats taught them. Then they would greet the visitors and peddle their wares, speaking all the while of the harmony they had found beneath the earth and their hatred of "Yellow Face," which was their name for the sun. Strictly celibate, they have dwindled in number. Occasionally you will see one emerge to prowl the famous "Underground Cafeteria," seeking converts among the tourists. But no worries— they are quickly chased away with Tasers.

THE KINGDOM OF CENTRAL PARK

Few now recall that New York's Central Park was initially in-

---

tended to be the capital of Frederick Law Olmsted's own utopian society: the great "Emerald Necklace" that would strangle the cities and ultimately return them to nature—or a kind of formal, sculptured, quasinatural state with a lot of gravel paths. In Olmsted's vision, all men and women were to wear waistcoats and evening gowns made of leaves. Everyone would learn to play the pan-pipes, talk to hawks, and live solely off the park's natural providence: wild ramps and mushrooms, chipmunks, and the petits-fours from Tavern on the Green. Colonies of Olmsted's kingdom were founded in Boston, Seattle, and elsewhere. But once his followers, largely drawn from the upper classes, tired of the revels and grass-wine and returned to their parlors, Olmsted abandoned the project and turned instead to the founding of the socialist republic known as Brookline, Massachusetts.

PEGLEG ISLAND

A colony in rural Wisconsin where it is believed that society's ills will be cured by forcing all members to act and dress like pirates. Eventually the pirates hope to take to the sea. For now they are constrained to a sixty-acre compound in the woods with only a small brook. There is a constant problem of moose trampling, due to that animal's known dislike of long red coats. But this, along with occasional scuffles with the live-action, role-playing gamers the next forest over, does not decrease their lusty love of life and incredibly fine work as looters and pillagers.

PANASONIC FARM

Founded in the 1860s in the spirit of thrift, equality, and polygamy, the Panasonics of Iowa supported themselves by making wooden air conditioners "to cool the skin and to dehumidify the passions." Panasonic air conditioners are still common today, but many do not know that when they enter a chilled room, their A/C unit was produced by people who believe that children should get high every third day.

HOW TO RAISE RABBITS FOR FOOD AND FUR:
THE UTOPIAN METHOD

—There shall be 54 perfectly square hutch groupings, each grouping housing no more than 6,000 rabbits, and no one grouping situated closer than 24 miles to any other.

—The hutches shall be rectangular and flat-roofed, and each shall house a family of 10 to 16 rabbits.

—Rabbit families with too many members shall have their offspring redistributed among all the hutches to maintain the correct number.

—Every 30 rabbit families shall be governed by a magistrate called a Syphogrant.

—The hutches shall be arranged contiguously, facing wide avenues on the front and sharing a garden in the back.

—Rabbits shall compete only through the beauty of their gardens.

—There shall be no private property; every 10 years the hutches shall be reassigned by lot.

—Gold and other precious metals shall have no meaning to the rabbits.

—Slavery is allowed among the rabbits. Criminal rabbits may choose to become slaves; but some slaves are free rabbits from neighboring rabbit communities who would prefer to be slaves in a utopian hutch than "free" in a traditional hutch. These latter rabbits are treated with respect by their masters.

—Rabbits shall practice at all times religious tolerance and commonly engage in a wide diversity of creeds and ceremonies.

—However, all rabbits shall believe in a single guiding entity that is eminently unknowable and synonymous with nature, called "Mithras."

—That said, there is some correlation between religious belief and rabbit weight (see table below).

—For this reason, whenever possible, it is wise to keep one or more Alfalfists in each hutch in hopes that they will convert the others through rational argument.

—Terminally sick rabbits may choose euthanasia, and this shall be considered noble and pleasant.

—All rabbits shall believe in a pleasant afterlife. Rabbits shall embrace death gladly and shall not be mourned when they pass, but celebrated. They will also be skinned and then either broiled or fried.

TABLE 17: WORSHIP V. WEIGHT TABLE FOR THE RAISING OF UTOPIAN RABBITS		
Religion	Average Wght: Buck	Average Wght: Doe
Carrot-sculpture idolatry	12 lbs, 4 oz	9 lbs, 2 oz
Asceticism	13 lbs, 1 oz	10 lbs, 6 oz
El-Arairah worship	13 lbs, 12 oz	10 lbs, 13 oz
Stool-of-ancestor worship	14 lbs, 1 oz	11 lbs, 3 oz
Episcopal—the cabbage and kale convention	14 lbs, 6 oz	11 lbs, 11 oz
Church of Rolled Oats	15 lbs, 7 oz	12 lbs, 5 oz
Alfalfists	16 lbs, 2 oz	12 lbs, 9 oz

LITTLE-KNOWN LAWS OF
TWO AMERICAN COMMUNITIES

1. Concord, Massachusetts, is a historic American town. Here sounded "the shot heard 'round the world," launching the American Revolution, and here was where Louisa May Alcott mysteriously crafted the exceedingly small men and women she used as her servants.

Some years ago I visited a friend who lived there, and apart from her unnerving cat, which drinks by dipping its paw into a dish of water in the same way a human would if he lacked a cup or glass, I found Concord to be a perfectly normal modern town that seemed to have forgotten its strange history. Long gone were the Transcendentalist gangs who used to cruise Monument Square night and day, drinking plum wine and loudly having spiritual intuitions. They have been replaced now by ordinary delinquents, whose insights can all be empirically (and boringly) proven.

I found this disappointing at first. But then I learned that Concord retains a number of unusual laws. How I discovered this, I am not allowed by the court to reveal. Suffice it to say that I learned it the hard way, over several nights in the Concord jail, until I could prove that I was not a man-sized South American monkey. And so the traveler would be wise to keep these little-known laws in mind:

—Grooming one's own hair shall not be allowed.

—Having insights by the pond shore at night or day shall be a crime.

—It is illegal for an unmarried man to keep a journal about his experiences in the woods around the pond.

—All cairn-building is asked to cease. The stones are needed elsewhere.

—Flutes or other musical instruments shall not be carved unless by a certified musical-instrument maker who keeps a residence in this town or another and does not live alone in the woods like a crazy person.

—Providing inspiration to self-appointed liberators of India, whether now or in the future, is forbidden.

—No man-sized South American monkeys may be housed in cabins.

—No one shall walk by moonlight with his giant trained monkey, advising children to be true first to themselves.

—Civil disobedience shall be punished by clubbing.

—Any prosperous person giving pies to people living in cabins by the pond shall also be clubbed.

—Tell none about the clubbings.

—Cabin burning shall not be a crime if it is done in the woods near the pond.

—The pitchforks are to be used only for hay- and giant monkey-stabbing. Particularly if that monkey may in fact be a warlock in monkey shape.

—If it is proven that one does not actually own a man-sized monkey, it shall not be considered a slander if the constable had previously made such claims. After all, what were we supposed to think, given your behavior, except to conclude that you sought to menace our town with a large monkey or ape who could hypnotize schoolchildren?

2. Some time after this experience, I was sent by a magazine to survey the malls of Minnesota, and so found myself at the Eden Prairie Center outside of Minneapolis.[47] I wanted to speak to the locals about their lives and aspirations, and before I was asked to leave I learned an interesting thing. A multimillion-dollar housing development had just been completed nearby: 77 quaint homes along curving private lanes that was called "The Concord, Massachusetts, Homes of Eden Prairie, Minnesota: A Private Community." Their re-creation of Concord, I was told, is rather stunning. They even have their own Walden Pond, although it is heated and kept indoors as part of the larger fitness and tranquility center. Yet it lacks two things: there is no mention anywhere of Thoreau's great experiment in the woods. And perhaps for this reason, none of the laws mentioned above are part of the community's charter. Except for one: Tell none about the clubbings. But as you know, this particular rule is common to most gated communities, so it may have been a coincidence.

WERE YOU AWARE OF IT?

The body of Thomas Edison was never buried. Instead, it was displayed for many decades in a traveling carnival . . . as an example of a Creek Indian!

DOES IT EVEN SEEM POSSIBLE!?

---

47. Please see "Secrets of the Mall of America," p. 64.

FOUR FAMOUS MONSTERS
AND THEIR HUNTERS

FORMER PEOPLE'S LIBERATION ARMY CORPORAL
HU ZHAO-HAN AND THE TIANCHI LAKE MONSTER

For more than a century, thousands of remote-volcanic-lake lovers have reported seeing a creature in Lake Tianchi, high in the Changbai Mountains of Northeastern China. All describe it as having a black, seal-like body, but descriptions of its head vary. Some say it has the head of a horse. Others say a bull. Others say a cat with a scaly face and horns.

None are correct, according to former People's Liberation Army Corporal Hu Zhao-Han. He saw it first eight years ago, when his unit passed the lake on routine maneuvers. He was seventeen at the time. On his next leave, he went back to the lake and saw the monster again. Thereafter, he deserted, building a small house by the lakeshore, to wait for the monster's return.

The army did not seem to mind that he deserted. Even among his most unsoldierly comrades-in-arms, Hu Zhao-Han was considered soft-limbed and odd, with a strange habit of staring at lamps and misplacing his meals. But he left behind his young wife, who apparently did mind, as she has since divorced him, and his newborn baby son, who does not enjoy that choice.

He now claims to see the monster "four to five evenings a week, at twilight."

"It has the head of a boy," he told Belgian reporter Aurelia Blix in 1998. "But it is small. Even for its small body, which is veritably seal-like, the head seems insignificant and pale. When he surfaces, his head is bald and as white as the moon, and his mouth is as round as the moon. He moves his mouth, but no sound comes out. He has the look of someone who has lost his place in a book, or of someone who has forgotten what he is going to say, and I am waiting for him to remember."

Often described as "China's Own Nessie," the Tianchi Lake Monster never attracted a cute Scottish name of its own. But former Cpl. Hu refers to it as "Shou-Liang," which translates roughly as "to reward, to forgive." I prefer "Little Shoulie."

JESSE LEE BOWEN AND THE NEW JERSEY DEVIL

As a child, Bowen first saw the cloven-hooved, wiry-haired, waist-high New Jersey Devil in the woods behind his home in Englewood. This was in 1900, when Englewood was still wild and dark and choked with forests that sheltered many creatures not typically seen in suburbs today, such as giant eagles and wild pigs and devils.

Despite historic rumors of baby theft, evil eye–giving, and other tricksterism, Bowen claimed that the Devil was generally well mannered, and mainly interested in backgammon. The Devil taught Bowen this most ancient of board games by moonlight, having originally learned it from the Sumerians themselves, and so they played together nightly, on a board of the Devil's own making (primarily constructed of nutshells and polished bone).

The Devil did not age, but Bowen grew up. And when he became a young man, he desired a fortune so that he could marry. The Devil did not have need for money, as his currency was pinecones and twigs, and his food the black air of night. Yet out of friendship and a desire for good backgammon, he agreed to Bowen's scheme: Every Saturday they would travel by boat to Manhattan. There the Devil would be displayed in a cage at the corner of Bowery and Spring. Inside the cage was a small table and devil-sized chair, and there the Devil would sit, playing backgammon via radiotelegraph with the greatest European players of the day. The Devil always won, but never understood the need for the cage.

"It is only 1920," Bowen explained. "America is not yet ready for a heroic demon, uncaged." He was, of course, correct, though this is obviously not true today.

Their partnership dissolved over this issue. Many years later, when Bowen was an old man (who never married, and whose autobiography, *Deal with the Devil*, was widely derided as fiction), he and the Devil once found each other sitting in the same compartment on the PATH train, and they did not even speak to each other.

DAN PAYTON AND THE SASQUATCH

Sasquatch hunters typically divide themselves into two camps:

Those in the first camp believe that there are only a handful of these famed bipedal mystery apes—most notably the "Bigfoot" of the Pacific Northwest, and the "Yeti" of the Himalayas—and for this reason, they believe, it is unlikely that any of them have ever met.

The second camp believes that there are many bigfoots, thriving throughout the United States, sometimes in small family-like groups, sometimes living in cars. This camp is larger, probably because it allows us to imagine what we have all suspected from birth: that bigfoot is just around the corner.

Dan Payton is of the latter school. In 1996, he attended the Fourth Greater Philadelphia Cryptozoology Convention. He carried with him an attaché case. In the case was a videocassette on which he claimed to have video-recorded a conversation he'd had with a Sasquatch he found living in the basement of the suburban Philadelphia high school where he was dean of discipline. He refused to screen the video, but he allowed a small group of experts to examine the attaché case. All they could report was that it seemed to have no hidden compartments.

Payton addressed the convention that evening in the Schuykill Ballroom. "I believe that for every U.S. citizen living today there is also a living Sasquatch," he told the astonished crowd. "In fact, based on my research, algorithms, and personal experience," he said as he soberly patted the attaché case, "I can conservatively conclude that there are probably more than four Sasquatches in this very room."

Thus began Payton's brief period of celebrity within Camp 2 of North America's bigfoot-hunting community. It would end several hours later, when, at the hotel bar, a Pittsburgh-based artist specializing in Chupacabra sculptures slipped the video out of Payton's attaché case and into the VCR behind the bar. It turned out to be an episode of

Leonard Nimoy's *In Search Of* . . . television program. The program did not even feature the Sasquatch (rather, it was on the Honey Island Swamp Monster). Payton claimed sabotage, probably by the Bigfoot himself, a theory immediately rejected by all at the bar. Everyone knows, they said, that the Sasquatch is too shy for sabotage.

But here is something of note. Later examination of hotel security camera archives revealed that when Payton made his famous pronouncement, a large hairy manlike creature (which almost certainly was not an elk or an ape) left the ballroom quickly, quietly, via the door near the coffee urns.

THE LOCH NESS MONSTER AND
COL. ROBERT WILSON

Here is the famous "Surgeon's Photo" of 1934, so named for Col. Robert Wilson, a respected London gynecologist, presumably because the term "Gynecologist's Photo" referred to something else at the time.

FIGURE 29: *The Surgeon's Photo*

But many now believe that Wilson never took this photo—that it was instead a hoax authored by famed charlatan Marmaduke Wetherell, who built a serpent's head of plastic wood, mounted it onto a toy submarine, and set it adrift in a pool of imitation water on an imaginary earth. All Marmaduke then needed was to present the photo under the name of a respected gynecologist and the hoax was complete. A fine story, so far as it goes, but I ask you: *plastic wood?* Let us be serious.

Here is the true story of the Colonel's unusual encounter with the Monster. The Colonel did indeed go to Loch Ness in April of 1934, for the first and only time, but he was not alone. A new road had recently been built to the Loch. And on this blacktop river a new stream of casual automobilers flowed to the water, and from it came a new torrent of sightings of the "monster" that had previously been seen only rarely, and largely only by Scottish people.

Most described a kind of sea snake, or perhaps an ancient plesiosaur. Fewer described a man-shaped Monster, tall-figured though by no means gigantic, with a tail easily concealed by ordinary trousers. But these few were correct: the Monster was only semi-aquatic, with webbed toes but otherwise normal digits, and a fine, silky fur covering his greenish skin.

History knows less of the gynecologist Colonel. We may or may not be accurate when we surmise that he had turned to cryptozoology because he was alone in the world: a widower, his children (self-delivered, naturally) grown and dispersed in typical human fashion. He came to the hunting of monsters as a hobby after a visit to New York City, where he observed a heated backgammon match between the New Jersey Devil and the Maharajah of Gaipajama. He could not bear to see the caged devil. He would prefer to see uncaged, monstrous majesty.

He first encountered the Monster in 1933 at The Tired Man, a historic London beer and meat pie establishment. The Monster had come to spend more and more of his time in London, as he was tired of Loch Ness, the new road, the constant scrutiny of the public, and his inability to meet the expectations of pilgrims expecting a swan-nish neck, a long body swooping in multiple humps above the mir-rorlike water's surface, and no trousers.

At The Tired Man, through the warm smoke haze and yellow firelight, the Monster spied the Colonel with his maps of the Loch, a heavy plate of steak and sheep's-heart pie, and the *Daily Mail.* The news that evening, as the Monster knew well, was the first, unillus-trated, report provided by the famed charlatan Marmaduke Wetherell, the self-styled big-game hunter hired by the *Mail* to find them a Nessie. As the Colonel turned the page again, the Monster could plainly read the headline, even in the dark of the pub, as his eyes were evolved to see in murky depths: THE LOCH NESS MONSTER: SERPENTINE CREATURE THAT LACKS JOY. He wished he could take the paper with his longish blue fingers and throw it into the fire. In-stead, he approached the Colonel politely and said, in a slightly gur-gling voice: "I will show you a better lie than that one." A plan was then hatched.

Now imagine it is April of 1934, and after many exchanged let-ters and mail-grams, they return to Loch Ness together. "It is day again," the Colonel tells the Monster on the midmorning train speeding Loch-wise to the north. "There are too many hours to fill, now that I am alone."

The Monster, opposite him in the otherwise empty compartment, refrains from saying, "Try being immortal."

Instead he drinks American whiskey from a flask, blissfully peat-free and tasting cleanly of beginnings: "To our endeavor," he says.

As they pull into the station, the Monster squints with his pupil-less eyes at the placard on the platform advertising Nessie Automo-bile Tours: a winking approximation of an aquatic dragon, cut out of wood, painted bright green, wearing a mischievous smile. Whoever is offering the tour has stepped away. "We alight here," says the Monster, "and we will hitch the rest of the way."

At Loch Ness that evening, the Colonel stands in inky water. He carries the wooden cutout of the dragon above the water as he walks. He wears waders he purchased for this purpose. Hodgman brand. (No relation.) He walks out until water coldly seeps down into his pants via his armpits, and then deeper still. He briefly considers not stopping, but does. Then he turns and arranges the wooden Nessie in the water, a swannish neck rising from the surface, a saurian head, peering westward. The Monster was correct: In silhouette, no one will see the grin. Soon the Colonel will walk out of the water a new man. A fraud.

Many years later, the BBC will trawl the lake with prying sonar and find no sort of monster at all. No one will find the abandoned wooden cutout. Gradually, belief in the Monster will fade with the photograph, and the Monster himself will never be seen in a London pub again. But the Surgeon's Photo is not the hoax that most people believe it to be.

Now the Colonel is in the water, and if we imagine correctly, he is thinking: This is a majestic fraud. And then there is the sound of a click upon the shore. The Monster modifies the camera's aperture with thin, blue fingers, checks his distance from the subject once more. Another click, and he's got it.

GOOD MORNING

As of this writing, this volume contains the entirety of COMPLETE WORLD KNOWLEDGE in the areas of my expertise.

Should more knowledge arise in the future, I shall consider gathering it in another volume for you.

But now, I think we are both tired. If you, like me, are a very slow reader, I imagine it is morning where you are. I trust the dawn looks different to you now—perhaps less magical, but also less frightening, now that you know it is the sun that is so warm and not lamps shone by demons atop your house.

Such is the effect of KNOWLEDGE upon the brain—a zinging clarity that does not quickly fade, but will last all the way to dinner, and then by bedtime will turn into awful, crushing dread.

I am grateful that you have read this book, and as we leave the range of each other's imaginary cameras, let me tell you that my clothes still do not fit, but I am much the better for this meeting all the same. I hardly know what to say except thank you, and also that I am very thin and good-looking, and I am wearing a powdered wig.

That is all.

A SPECIAL BONUS EXCERPT
FROM MY NEXT BOOK

One thing you have perhaps read about in the news is that I am now the father of a human child. I have not discussed this in *The Areas of My Expertise* for reasons of privacy, and also to preserve the integrity of my next book and its inevitable profits. I did not wish to write this next book, but one can only duck the law for so long. As a writer and as a parent, I was reminded by several constabulary notices stamped to my door that I am now required to devote my creative life solely to writing about my daughter—how brilliant and beautiful she is, and how her naïve wisdom and amusing antics have changed the way I look at life.

Everyone, I am sure, will find this fascinating.

And so I am pleased to offer this preview of my next book, which will collect my wacky anecdotes of fatherhood, touching tales of my daughter's babyhood, and all the charming wit and wisdom of me at my finest.

I have not settled on a title yet. But like every good writer, I have a lot of ideas on how the jacket should look.

It will have a picture of me on it. I will be dressed casually, maybe wearing a cozy sweater. And I will be smiling with bemused exhaustion. And I will probably be touching my chin with two fingers, as if to say "I am contemplating the unique brilliance and beauty of my infant daughter, and soon you will be doing the same."

There will not be a picture of my daughter on the cover. I would like her to have some semblance of a childhood before she inevitably becomes a famous public personality like her father; so to protect her privacy, I will refer to my daughter herewith only as "Hodgmina."

It will be a very readable book, full of stories told in a conversational style, and often in sentence fragments, as if I am right there in the room with you. I hope you will not find this spooky.

To give you an idea of how this will work, I would like to share a few short chapters with you now from my new book, tentatively titled either *Hodgmina: American Baby, American Life* . . .

or *A Child Called It* . . .

or *What I Have Learned from the Young Woman Who Lives in Our House and Claims to Be Our Daughter.*

This from the introduction, "Why Children Are Better Than Monkeys":

> Children are better than monkeys for several reasons. One reason is that they are not yammering away in sign language all the time. Before the age of two, many of them do not even know the English language. The other reasons that children are better than monkeys are secret, but you can read about them in my book.

This is from Chapter 12, "The Limits of Children":

> I have learned that newborn infants roll their eyes around and move their heads and their arms in short jerky spasms. And if you homeschool them, they will stay this way forever. But this makes it difficult to train them in fencing or bartending or any of the other great defensive arts.

The is the entirety of Chapter 19, "What About Badminton?":

> When I say that Hodgmina is brilliant, and when I tell people about her guest sermon last Sunday at St. John the Divine, and her surprising skills at badminton, people want to know: is she a child prodigy?
>
> I reply: I hope not. There is too much pressure put on children. They should have time to explore and enjoy the world as children, and not be forced into the highly competitive badminton circuit. Unless the child really wants that, and has signaled as much by crying or pooping.
>
> Basically, it comes down to this: Child prodigies are fine, but I could do without all the violins. If you have ever been alone at night in Penn Station, barefoot, with only a sword cane and a half-empty bottle of brandy, and suddenly, swiftly, with ninja-like stealth, a group of child prodigies surrounds you, rattling their violin cases, you will know what I am talking about.

This is from Chapter 47, "Some Children Cannot Walk":

> I have learned that many children who are only four months old have difficulty walking. This makes it nearly impossible to send them on even the simplest errands. For example, I recently asked Hodgmina to go to the pharmacy and get Daddy's special medicine. She replied by jerking her hands around a lot and then farting. I explained that it was OK, the pharmacist knows Daddy very well, and if the pharmacist is in the

back sleeping on his little army cot again, just go behind the counter and take whatever you need. Then she started to cry. I never could bear a woman's tears. So I said: fine. I instead wrote a note to the pharmacist, pinned it to Hodgmina's dickey, and handed her to a passing vagrant who I hoped knew the way.

This is the entirety of Chapter 82, "Dress-Up Time!":

It is hard to find fishing waders or a suit of armor that will fit a four-month-old human child.

Luckily, children love hand-me-downs. You can give them all the clothing that you don't wear anymore, like your dickey. (Although the fact in this case is that I rarely wore my dickey, and I had often found myself wondering why I ever bought it.) But now it is hers, like so many of my old shirts and hats and daggers and cuff links. Hodgmina *loves* the cuff links, especially after I taught her how exciting it is to put two or three in your mouth and run around the living room.

But it's not just clothes. You can also give children other things you don't have use for anymore, such as your kerosene lanterns, most of your belts, whatever residual knowledge you may have of French literary theory, and your optimism. I used to believe, for example, that you had to spend money to make money. This is obviously not true. But now, Hodgmina be-lieves it. And I find this to be charming.

Hodgmina was just saying it the other day,

and I was quite moved. I looked into her eyes as they rolled about in her head and said, "Hodgmina, you are a dreamer. Keep dreaming! For the sake of our planet's future, I hope you never lose your childlike idealism. But at the same time, I hope it does not get in my way."

If you wish to buy *Untitled Book About Hodgmina,* just "clip 'n' send" the form on page 229 to me at P.O. Box 1618 Cathedral Station, New York, NY 10025. They'll make sure that you receive lots of information about all the other books I might be publishing and some of the exciting new debt-consolidation schemes I might be marketing.

Also, if I ever finish my book on Hodgmina, they will probably let you know. After clipping out the form, please also be sure to buy another copy of *The Areas of My Expertise,* as this one is obviously ruined.

YES! By taping a hobo nickel to this form I am indicating that I would like to receive more information about books by John Hodgman and also other books and debt-consolidation schemes.

NAME

STREET

CITY

STATE

ZIP +4 CODE

COUNTRY

AGE (OPTIONAL)

E-MAIL ADDRESS (OPTIONAL)

POLL QUESTION—*flight or invisibility?*
(optional; please do not write in alternate superpowers):

TAPE HOBO NICKEL HERE!

TABLE 18: EXPERTS CONSULTED DURING THE PREPARATION OF THIS BOOK

The 215 Festival		on the subject of Philadelphia
Lee K.	Abbott	on the subject of thriving
Mark	Adams	on the subject of Chicago
Charles	Barbee	on the subject of *Silent Running*
Maribeth	Batcha	on the subject of burning coal mines
Alex	Blumberg	on the subject of magnetic recording devices
Patrick	Borelli	on the subject of seagulls
Arthur	Bradford	on the subject of guitar demolition
Lynnda	Butler	on the subject of skunks as pets
Bruce	Campbell	on the subject of fake blood
Art	Chung	on the subject of dungeons
Doctor Cocktail		on the subject of nonalcoholic gin
Simon	Collins	on cosh pockets
Christine	Connor	or possibly "Connors"
Elizabeth	Connor	of the art department
Margaret	Cordi	on the subject of current events
Jonathan	Coulton	on computer programs
Mike	Daisey	on the subject of Korean cuisine
Josh and Jason	Dean and Adams, respectively	on the subject of Peter Frampton
Dale	DeGroff	on the subject of salooning
Joseph	DiPietro	no idea
Dave	Eggers	on the subject of giraffes
Robert	Elmes	on the Galápagos Islands
Devin	Emke	on midnight baseball
Blake	Eskin	on the subject of political lists
The staff of Essentials, Northampton		on the subject of perfect objects
Jason	Evans	Mayor of Coolidge Corner
Kassie	Evashevski	on the subject of magicians v. detectives
The Amazing Duo of Flansburgh and Goldwasser on cocktails that women enjoy		
Devin	Friedman	on the subject of other peoples' stories
Elizabeth	Gilbert	on the subject of lobsters in Maine
Magus Peter H.	Gilmore	on the subject of Satan
Ira	Glass	on the subject of wireless communication

TABLE 18: EXPERTS CONSULTED
DURING THE PREPARATION OF THIS BOOK *continued*

Neil	Gordon	on the subject of digital photography
Damon	Graff	of the Graff Institute
Gavin	Grant	on the subject of printing presses
Brendan	Greeley	on the subject of Germany
Eric	Grossman	on the subject of mekons
Emmanuel	Haldeman-Julius	of Girard, Kansas
The firm of Handelman and Guion representing the estate of Dick Cockburn		
Anna	Henchman	on the subject of cats drinking with their paws
Christine	Hill	on the subject of accounting
Dave	Hirmes	on the subject of artificial ice
Lucy	Hodgman	on the subject of lobsters in New York City
Cynthia	Hopkins	on the subject of holy water
Samantha	Hunt	on the subject of Nikola Tesla
Richard	Jeffrey	on the subject of cybermen
Lady Killigrew		on the subject of coffee and fine sandwiches
Starlee	Kine	on the subject of ghosts
Geoff	Kloske	on the subject of foreign nations
Chuck	Klosterman	on the subject of Billy Joel
Jon	Langford	of the foreign accent guild
Lisa	Leingang	on the subject of bourbon and 7-Up
The Library of Congress and its staff of expert scanners		
Kelly	Link	on the subject of Northampton, Mass.
Brett	Martin	on the subject of chopped liver
Sean	McDonald	on the subject of patience
Eugene	Mirman	on the subject of the Russian space program
Vanessa	Mobley	who once observed my child peeing in the middle of Flatbush Avenue
The Montague Bookmill, "books you don't need in a place you can't find"		
Rachelle	Nashner	on the subject of elks and insurance
The North American Almanac		The Aristocrat of Alamanacs
The Other Page		on the subject of eels
Whitney	Pastorek	on schoolyard divination techniques
Alexander	Payne	on the subject of the stockyards
Tom	Perrotta	on haircuts and their history

TABLE 18: EXPERTS CONSULTED
DURING THE PREPARATION OF THIS BOOK *continued*

Neal	Pollack	the renowned parenting expert
Sam	Potts	on the subjects of doppelgangers, Fritz Lang, and Saturdays
William	Poundstone	on the subject of big secrets
Todd	Pruzan	on the subject of the clumsy people of Europe
Adam	Rapoport	on the subject of foie gras
David	Rees	on diseases of the horse
Lindsay	Robertson	on mass communication
Adam	Sachs	on the subject of E.L. Wisty
John	Sellers	on the subject of Bruce Campbell
Allison	Silverman	on the history of the atomic bomb
Elizabeth	Skurnick	of Baltimore
Ken	Smith	on the subject of white-squirrel towns v. black-squirrel towns
Elizabeth	Spiers	on the subject of wolves
Joel	Stein	on the subject of Princeton University
Lorin	Stein	on the subject of the Gramercy Park Hotel
Daniel	Stewart	on the subject of dragons
Darin	Strauss	on the subject of the long-form confidence game
Brian	Tart	on the subject of twins
Hannah	Tinti	on the life cycle of rabbits
A tip o' the hat to Ben Schott		
Paul	Tough	on the subject of alien contact
Sarah	Vowell	motivational speaker specializing in encouragement at critical times
The Wallaces and Wallechinsky		on the subject of lists, books, and books of lists, and also Chang and Eng
Bill Wasik and the research staff of "Volume 13" on the subject of encyclopedias		
Dr. P. Thurston	Wikipedia	on the subject of the United States
David	Wondrich	world-famous George Washington impersonator
The World Alamanac Book of the Strange		on Sasquatch
Ryan, your bartender		beard expert

TABLE 19: IMAGE CREDITS

Omen Tabulation Pool	Library of Congress, Prints & Photographs Division, LC-USZ62-101229
An Ominous Portent	Lynnda Butler
Playthings of the Mermen	Library of Congress, Prints & Photographs Division, LC-DIG-cwpbh-01955
Typical Cyborg Mischief	© BBC, Courtesy the BBC
Can You Describe . . .	Library of Congress, Prints & Photographs Division, LC-USZ6-1041
Deep Owls	Library of Congress, Prints & Photographs Division, Prokudin-Gorskii Collection, LC-DIG-prokc-20702
Prepare to Tip Extra . . .	Library of Congress, Prints & Photographs Division, LC-USZ62-126527
Senate Pages . . .	Library of Congress, Prints & Photographs Division, LC-DIG-ppmsca-09408
Georgian Woman Standing . . .	Library of Congress, Prints & Photographs Division, Prokudin-Gorskii Collection, LC-DIG-prokc-21598
Hodgman waders	Courtesy Hodgman
Albert Shame . . .	Library of Congress, Prints & Photographs Division, LC-DIG-cwpbh-02306
The Lobster	Bernard Landgraf; a transparent copy is available here: http://commons.wikimedia.org/wiki/ Image:Fischotter%2C_Lutra_Lutra.JPG
Another Stumper	Library of Congress, Prints & Photographs Division, LC-USZ6-1044
"The Hobo Standard"	courtesy Barbados
Secretary of the Treasury . . .	Library of Congress, Prints & Photographs Division, LC-DIG-ggbain-00034

TABLE 19: IMAGE CREDITS *continued*	
The Hobo Vogue	Library of Congress, Prints & Photographs Division, LC-USZC2-1130
Herbert Hoover…	Library of Congress, Prints & Photographs Division, LC-USZ62-111716
"awesome hedge maze"	Courtesy Jordan Greywolf, http://greywolf.critter.net/
Ready for Negotiation	Library of Congress, Prints & Photographs Division, LC-USZC4-8658
Historical Fisticuffs	Library of Congress, Prints & Photographs Division, LC-USZ62-10364
A Despicable Habit	Library of Congress, Prints & Photographs Division, LC-USZ62-131903
"Let's Use My Ferret . . ."	Library of Congress, Prints & Photographs Division, LC-DIG-ggbain-00034
The Great Seal . . .	by the great Elizabeth Connor, after a traditional design
Only the Bourbon Cask . . .	Library of Congress, Prints & Photographs Division, LC-USZ62-58072
Formed by Masonic Ritual?	photo taken by Bill Jack Rodgers for the U.S. Government, courtesy Los Alamos National Laboratory, with thanks to Dan Comstock
Here Is a Familiar Sight	DoD photo by Tech. Sgt. Andy Dunaway
Now Look at the Same City . . .	courtesy the Church of Satan, www.churchofsatan.com
T. R., an Asthmatic . . .	White House Historial Association (White House Collection)
The Surgeon's Photo	The Daily Mail

That is all.